EQUIPPING MEN FOR SPIRITUAL BATTLE

Equipping Men for
Spiritual Battle

Max Heine

VINE
BOOKS

Servant Publications
Ann Arbor, Michigan

Unless otherwise noted, all quotations from the New
Testament and Old Testament except for the Psalms are from
The Holy Bible, New International Version. Copyright © 1973,
1978, 1983 International Bible Society. Used by permission of
Zondervan Bible Publishers.

Vine Books is an imprint of Servant Publications especially
designed to serve Evangelical Christians.

Published by Servant Publications
P.O. Box 8617
Ann Arbor, Michigan 48107

Cover design Gerald L. Gawronski

93 94 95 96 97   10 9 8 7 6 5 4 3 2 1

Printed in the United States of America

ISBN 0-89283-842-6

Library of Congress Cataloging-in-Publication Data

Heine, Max, 1952-
    Equipping men for spiritual battle / Max Heine.
    p. cm.
    "Vine Books."
    ISBN 0-89283-842-6
    1. Men—Religious life. 2. Husbands—Religious life.
3. Spiritual warfare. 4. Christian life—1960- I. Title.
BV4528.2.H45   1993
248.8'42—dc20
                                            93-35776

Dedication

To Aaron, Benjamin, Connor, and Dustin.
May you fight the good fight of faith,
and take hold of the eternal life
to which you were called (1 Timothy 6:12).

ACKNOWLEDGMENTS

I AM INDEBTED to Bill Thrasher, Mike and Kathy Perren, William Scroggins, Hal Threadcraft, Keith and Roberta Hess, Joseph Wheat, Robert Morgan, Lucian Croft, Tom White, Bruce Longstreth, Dave Masoner, and Pete Peters. These friends, pastors, and counselors willingly took time out of their busy lives to share their thoughts about spiritual warfare and men's issues. Many of their experiences and insights fill these pages. Without them, this book would lack much.

Contents

Men of War

O UT OF THE MANY STATUES that decorate our nation's capital, two heroes from the Civil War especially intrigue me: Union General George Brinton McClellan and Thomas J. "Stonewall" Jackson, a Confederate general. McClellan sits tall in the saddle, surveying the scene, his horse alert. Jackson sits low in the saddle, his horse panting in exhaustion, nostrils inflated.

These depictions suggest two distinctly different men of war. While the two fought for opposing sides, something else sets them apart. You can see it in the statues, but don't be fooled. It's not the untouched McClellan symbolizing Union victory, the bedraggled Jackson representing Confederate loss. I'm talking about less tangible qualities: their attitudes, their ways of viewing war, their willingness to do what they were called to do with an integrity that transcends fleeting victories and defeats. As Christian men in the midst of a different sort of war, we can learn much from their example.

WAR GAMES

By his mid-thirties, General George Brinton McClellan had amassed a stellar military record. When President Lincoln put him in charge of the rag-tag army defending Washington, the dashing general went right to work. He kept the soldiers out of the bars and whorehouses and put them through several hours a day of military drill.

More and more volunteers arrived to swell the troops to over 100,000. As the Army of the Potomac took shape, McClellan staged grandiose reviews. Boisterous sounds of bands, drums, and marching filled the air. The public began to admire the general as much as did his men, who were grateful for the pride he had instilled. Newspapers began to call McClellan, a longtime admirer of Napoleon, "Little Napoleon." The general encouraged more of the same.[1]

McClellan planned to launch a three-pronged assault as his troops drove south. But months passed, and the fine-tuned army went nowhere. Newspapers mocked McClellan's reports of "all's quiet." Republicans in Congress fretted that Europe would perceive the Union's inactivity as weakness and decide to endorse the Confederacy.

Informed of the proximity of 150,000 Confederate soldiers, McClellan continued to balk, even though other sources assured him the estimate was inflated. In fact, only about fifty thousand troops were anywhere near Washington. But the Union general preferred caution to conflict. Perhaps spooked by sightings of rebel cannons that later turned out to be black-log decoys, McClellan insisted that he needed 270,000 soldiers to attack. Confiding in his wife that the failure to accomplish anything certainly was not his fault, the Union general eventually took his army into winter quarters.[2]

Were this but one mistake, it would not be worth noting. But the remainder of the war reflected the same pattern. McClellan, for all his preparation for war, shied away from its execution. His *modus operandi* proved to be one of cautiously waiting to attack, convincing himself that he was outnumbered when he wasn't, retreating unnecessarily, asking for more volunteers, and disobeying Lincoln's express orders to pursue the enemy. Yet the general's letters reveal that he continually considered himself the savior of the Union. He sloughed off blame for lost opportunities like a snake shedding its skin.

A war raged close at hand, but you wouldn't have known it from watching George Brinton McClellan. In fact, the war dragged on and on, partly because vacillating Union leadership like McClellan's was matched against the scrappy tenacity of Confederate officers such as Thomas J. Jackson, a man who seemed born for war.

PURSUIT OF WAR

Why did the creator of Jackson's statue portray him and his horse in a state of exhaustion? The general was known to march his troops great distances to pursue Union forces, who often had him far outnumbered, and then to press his attack as far as he could. Jackson believed the war and his role in it to be divine appointments. Consider these three accounts:[3]

- When Confederates were losing to Union forces at the first battle of Bull Run, Jackson's brigade held its position—earning him the nickname "Stonewall." His stand marked the turning point in the battle, reversing an apparent Northern victory into a humiliating rout.

- Jackson pushed his men through a two-day, fifty-six-mile march around John Pope's right flank to cut his rail line to Washington and loot his supply depot. Pope finally thought he had nailed the Confederate troops in a vulnerable position and attacked. When Jackson's men ran low on ammunition, they began hurling rocks and still managed to hold their position against strong odds.

- In a little over a month during the Shenandoah Valley campaign, Jackson's men "marched almost four hundred miles, inflicted seven thousand casualties, seized huge quantities of badly needed supplies, kept almost forty thousand Federal troops off the Peninsula—frightened the North and inspired the South."

"TO PRAY AND TO FIGHT"

This little history lesson serves not to vilify McClellan or enshrine Jackson. Neither man's record was black or white. A Mexican War hero, McClellan had been second in his class at West Point. He had authored manuals on military tactics and showed an obvious knack for instilling great morale in his troops.[4] And Jackson, for all his religious zeal, seemed to love war more than the warriors. He would drive his men to the point of collapse and even seemed insensitive to their deaths. While no doubt sincere, his Christianity seemed rigid and misguided.

In the context of this book, these two men offer two very distinct attitudes during one common event: war. One manifested a constant awareness of the battle, an eagerness to fight even when outnumbered, along with a disregard for the sacrifice involved. The other showed a reluctance to initiate combat, even when holding a superior position.

Unfortunately, Christian men in our day display the same divergent approaches to the war between God's way and Satan's. It's all too easy for us to become actively involved with the things we see—jobs, material possessions, and family concerns—and remain passive to the things unseen, the things of the spirit.

God may have stirred us enough to attend church, and perhaps even to serve within the church. But how easily we convince ourselves that we're fighting for God when we're still milling about the camp. How often do we become absorbed in the pageantry of attractive church programs, impressive buildings, glorious choirs, fine Sunday clothes, and escalating budgets and attendance? Are we much different than McClellan, who loved to stage his spectacles of polished marching troops and bands, who knew military theory well enough to write manuals, but who resisted putting it into practice, who kept calling for more and more people to feed his ever-expanding army that rarely faced off against the enemy?

Jackson summed up man's "entire duty" in four words: "to pray and fight."[5] In a nutshell, that's what this book is about. We're going to look at the kind of fighting that goes hand in hand with prayer. Our weapons don't depend on bullets, blades, or bombs. As the apostle Paul put it, "The weapons we fight with are not the weapons of the world. On the contrary, they have divine power to demolish strongholds" (2 Corinthians 10:4).

But before focusing on this invisible, powerful weaponry, you need to realize that warfare in the spiritual realm is not optional. Spiritual warfare is a fact of life. In the ongoing struggle between good and evil, Satan wants nothing more than to inflict maximum harm on God's people. He is out to ruin you in body, mind, and spirit. Consider the array of ordinary situations that often boil down to a spiritual contest:

- You find a female office co-worker so warm, so understanding of your problems, that you think about her more than your wife.

- You fret over your teenage daughter who insists on running with a bad crowd instead of her old friends in the church youth group.

- A sudden avalanche of major car and appliance repair bills threatens to plunge you into debt for a long time.

- Even though the quality of your work has improved, your boss has begun to belittle you in subtle ways.

- Your wife complains that you don't express your inner feelings enough, but you feel like you're communicating as much as you can.

- Your best friend has become less and less able to control his drinking problem.

- You sensed months ago that you needed a daily devotional time, but you've been unable to fit it into your busy schedule.

Perhaps you thought these kinds of problems were just life. Think again. Such hot spots may be evidence of a much bigger struggle, just as sporadic volcanic eruptions offer a glimpse into the mass of molten rock buried deep beneath the earth's crust. In the face of such difficulties, God is looking for men who see their duty as praying and fighting.

WHAT WAR?

Do you approach life with a minimalist attitude? In your job, do you settle for the easiest work with the least responsibility, or do you seek out challenges that will test your mettle and perhaps lead to a promotion? If you play on a softball team, are you satisfied to sit on the bench and watch your teammates make the big plays, or are you willing to risk failure by getting out on the field? When you commit yourself to a regular exercise program, do you exert the least energy possible, or do you push yourself beyond your personal comfort level?

Our call in Christ involves much the same choices. When you accepted Christ as your Savior, you may have been thinking more in terms of buying an after-life insurance policy with easy, low premiums, rather than volunteering to take your untrained body onto a battlefield bursting with gunfire and flying shrapnel.

If the idea of personal challenge has never entered your vision of the Christian walk, don't be surprised if you haven't heard bullets whizzing by your skull. Perhaps your level of resistance has been so weak that Satan has concentrated his efforts elsewhere. Or perhaps you simply have not ventured into the thick of the fray, whatever the reason may be.

God has chosen you because of his mercy, not because of your kind offer to try to be a nice guy (see Ephesians 1). And God's call to follow him means that he has plans for you. He knows about the war raging in the spiritual realm. God's intention is that the entire church throughout all the ages would help to bring about the eternal triumph of righteousness.

In the opposing corner glowers Satan, a lover of evil who has targeted the human race for spiritual warfare. He has two general goals. One goal is *to keep unbelievers in a state of darkness.* Satan wants to keep those who don't know God shielded from the light of the gospel, enslaved to sin, ever struggling to pursue any perceived route to happiness, as long as it doesn't pertain to God. The other goal is *to weaken the faith of believers* by utilizing his primary method: deception. While satanic subterfuge takes many forms, it is all designed to make us doubt God and the Bible, place trust in ourselves, rationalize our moral compromises, overestimate the pleasures of sin, and hide any evidence of weakness and failure.

We men are capable of entertaining enormous deception! When McClellan learned that the wounded Confederate General Joseph E. Johnston was to be replaced by General Robert E. Lee as commander-in-chief, he was pleased. He wrote that Lee "is too cautious and weak under grave responsibility— personally brave and energetic to a fault, he yet is wanting in moral firmness when pressed by heavy responsibility and is likely to be timid and irresolute in action."[6]

McClellan, of course, had described himself to a tee. But in his vanity and self-deception, he had laid his bad rap on Lee, a military leader who proved to be anything but cautious, weak, timid, or irresolute. There's a little bit of McClellan in most men. Privately overconfident of our perceived abilities, we either blind ourselves to our shortcomings or pin the blame on someone else. And whenever part of our human nature willingly accedes to Satan's wiles, spiritual warfare becomes even more challenging.

AN OLD WAR

Let's briefly review the origins of the war in which we find ourselves embroiled. At some point in pre-history, Satan rebelled against God and took some other angels with him. As soon as God began his creation, this fallen angel started looking for ways to mess it up. He didn't have to look far.

Eve fell prey to the smooth talk of Satan, who appeared to her in the form of a serpent. The woman then passed the forbidden fruit to Adam, who knowingly disobeyed God as he sampled the contraband. When God confronted the couple, Adam replied, "The woman you put here with me—she gave me some fruit from the tree, and I ate it" (Genesis 3:12).

The first recorded sin paints a clear picture of man's penchant for dodging responsibility for his own actions. We see this tendency to pass the buck repeated later in Scripture, a weakness which seriously complicates man's role in spiritual warfare. It's hard to achieve victory when you can't admit that you're losing the battle and by your own fault.

After sin had entered the world, God addressed Satan: "And I will put enmity between you and the woman, and between your offspring and hers; he will crush your head, and you will strike his heel" (Genesis 3:15). The strong language removes any possible doubt that spiritual warfare had been declared: *enmity, crush, strike.* From that point on, a line of unrighteous offspring consistently opposed the line of righteous seed.

Throughout all of the Old Testament, we see this war raging between the two seeds, with their spiritual lineage either in God or Satan. God's chosen people kept falling again and again. They would sin and repent, sin and repent. Scripture ascribes sins and blemishes to even the most highly regarded of the Old Testament figures, such as Moses and David, themselves victims of spiritual warfare. Meanwhile, the Hebrews looked for the day when their seed would produce the "skull-crusher" prophesied in Genesis 3:15, the one who would put Satan in his place once and for all.

Finally, the longed-for one arrived: Jesus Christ, the Messiah. By his death and resurrection, Christ sealed the ultimate defeat of Satan. However, the battle over the human race drags on. Having been allowed by God a large measure of dominion over the earth, Satan has inflicted plenty of damage. Because God's final plan for all of history has not yet culminated, Satan continues to thrash about, to enjoy his limited dominion.

Gifted with keen insight, Satan knows how to tempt us in our most vulnerable areas. If so, does he also know that he's eventually doomed? I think so. When Jesus confronted the violent Gadarene demoniac (Matthew 8:28-29), the demons inquired through the man, "Have you come here to torture us before the appointed time?" They knew that a day of judgment lurked somewhere in the future. So why do Satan and his legions prolong a war they know they can't win? Satan is merely being true to his character: he wants to pervert, to destroy, to kill.

I can begin to understand his motivation from watching my four sons. When I tell a younger one to return a toy to the older brother who owns it, I rarely see the object politely handed over. He usually dashes the thing on the ground, or hurls it far away, or best yet, aims it right at the unsuspecting owner with enough velocity to wrench a little pain. In other words, impending justice does not necessarily change a sour heart. Although subject to God's justice and control over history, Satan sees no need to tone down his act.

NOT JUST SURVIVING

"Fine," you may say. "This ongoing struggle against evil is precisely why our church hires a full-time pastor and why we have extra prayer meetings in addition to Sunday services—for those who have more patience than I'll ever have for just sitting there and praying."

Satan would love for you to leave it at that. Delegate fighting the war to someone else, and he'll have no trouble looting your little corner. Believe me, the devil does not have your best interests at heart. God is the one who loves you and has a wonderful plan for your life. What exactly does Satan plan for you?

- To make you doubt God and expect little of him.
- To make prayer dull and boring, and reading the Bible as appealing as if it were in the original Hebrew and Greek.
- To discourage you from being a spiritual leader in your home.
- To break up your marriage.
- To alienate your children from you and thwart the establishment of godly convictions in their lives.
- To keep you and other men out of spiritual matters and thereby derail growth of the kingdom of God.
- To intimidate you from witnessing about your faith.
- To tempt you to compromise your integrity on the job.

And that's just for starters, but you can begin to see what sort of marbles are up for grabs. What if you read this list and think, "Gosh, I've been a Christian for years and I never felt there was any evil force trying to do all that stuff to me!" I have bad news for you. It's not that Satan has let you off the hook; more than likely he's been picking your pocket and you haven't reached for your wallet lately.

If some items on this list ring a bell, then you know the war is real. As soon as you said yes to Christ, you said no to Satan. Their enmity predates Adam, but the line was drawn in earth's dust back in Genesis 3:15. God and Satan know which side of the line you're on.

But then it's not just a matter of being on the right side. If you're a man, you probably like to compete. And the only thing you like better than competing is winning. I live in Tuscaloosa, Alabama, whose residents know no greater joy than watching our native University of Alabama Crimson Tide football team humiliate an opponent. Victory is much sweeter than defeat in spiritual warfare as well. After all, you've already enlisted. The enemy has been taking shots at you. Wouldn't you rather come out not just a survivor, but a winner? I know I would. Of course, it helps to know who—or what—you're up against.

One of my younger sons has been fond of announcing that he's having a "bad day." If he seems to be in a grouchy mood and I lay down some limits on his behavior, bingo! He's having a **Bad Day**, which he expresses with all the tears and grimaces worthy of an Academy Award.

Men are a bit more resilient, usually requiring more than one catastrophe to make a bad day. News that your car needs an eight-hundred-dollar engine job (and it needed it yesterday) strikes with unqualified horror. You can moan about this blow to your checkbook and garner some sympathy from your friends, but it doesn't carry the same weight as an unbelievable flurry of harassments that pile up within one twenty-four-hour period. That's a truly bad day.

But does it indicate spiritual warfare? Not necessarily. Not every contrary experience comes straight from the devil. Later chapters will clarify the fine line between trial, temptation, and testing. You may never know whether a spiritual dimension explained your coming down with a cold on the first day of your vacation. But when that cold sets in and you feel cheated, you can bet God has an interest in how you handle yourself and how you treat those around you.

Regardless of where life's trials originate, we all know that they come in abundance. Major or minor troubles can be like a flurry of "flaming arrows," to use the Bible's imagery. Only a small percentage of those arrows need to be effective for Satan to make the bottom line of your bad day equal spiritual defeat. Fortunately, God empowers each of his children to thwart any attempts of the enemy.

At the same time, remember that God's ultimate interest is not in ranking your degree of outward success as a spiritual warrior. There's no rating system you must qualify under in order to stay in the game.

Rather, the Lord's watching to see if you will be faithful enough to keep fighting in your own battlefield—and he's empowered you with the courage to do so. He's eagerly waiting for you to take up your spiritual armor and weaponry. Further, he's made available exactly what you need for the conflicts that surround you. He's longing for you to admit your limitations. Trust that he'll provide the grace within you and his church outside of you as the best sources of power you could ever want. Are you ready to move ahead?

Enemy Tactics

EARLY 1948. Desperately outnumbered, the Jews found themselves locked in a brewing struggle with the Arabs. The point of contention: what group would control Jerusalem after the imminent departure of the British.

The Jewish underground militia anticipated a crucial development in conjunction with the British evacuation. Haganah officer Nahum Stavy understood the stakes all too well. The British held a vital compound of buildings in the northeastern fringe of Jewish Jerusalem. Whichever side seized this compound would achieve a major advantage in gaining control of the city.

One problem loomed large, however. The British planned to issue little or no notice of the evacuation. Stavy met with a key British major, explaining that it would mean so much to keep in touch. The major pointed out that two thousand dollars would work wonders to jog his memory when a certain time came.

Early one morning, the major called Stavy with this message: "Be outside the gate at ten o'clock with the money." After a quick tour of the buildings in question, two thousand dollars purchased a ring of keys to supplement the critical information. Only fifteen minutes later, the British were gone, the Jewish militia had occupied the strategic compound, and the Arabs were vainly attacking what would become the Haganah's primary base in Jerusalem.[1]

Military intelligence plays a critical role in determining who takes home the spoils after a battle. The man who wants to assume his proper role in spiritual warfare also needs all the military intelligence he can get, particularly concerning his enemy: Satan and his demons. Whether in business, sports, or military action, two general pathways lead to information about a competitor or enemy. One is the school of hard knocks, otherwise known as experience. The second is studying the available data. The more you make use of the second way, the less painful the first is likely to be.

In order to learn more about the Enemy of God and his people, we'll study the three primary strategies employed by Satan: deception, accusation, and destruction. We'll also examine men's susceptibility to those tactics.

THE CON JOB

During and after the 1991 Gulf War, American pop culture seized upon a phrase coined by Iraq's Saddam Hussein: "Mother of all battles." Talk show hosts, newspaper columnists, and advertisers soon began to express any superlative as the "Mother of all ———."

Long before Saddam's pompous wartime prediction, Jesus revealed a similar superlative about his eternal enemy, Satan: "He is a liar and the father of lies." This figures. If God is truth, as the Bible says, then his enemy could find no basis for conflict by using truth. Ah, but a *mixture*—truth and lies, truth and distortions, truth and select omissions—could work wonders. The father of lies has whispered these sorts of concoctions to countless men:

- Your sexual drive is at its peak while you're young (true). Your single friends from work are sleeping with their girlfriends (probably true). God is so pleased that you've been chaste thus far (true), and you know you'll be faithful to your wife once you're married (true, you hope), so it's no big deal to have a little fun now (false).

- You pay so much in taxes (true) that you really don't need to file Social Security taxes on your household help (false). Hardly anyone else does (true).

- That was your favorite tie (true)! You paid too much for it (true). You've told your three-year-old to stay out of your closet (true). And you've told him to never touch the felt-tipped markers (true). He needs discipline (true) and you've got every right to whop that little bottom a few extra times with a little extra muscle (false). And sprinkling a few profanities at high volume might help to enforce the discipline (false). It would sure make you feel better (true, at least momentarily).

- Your sexual relationship with your wife has never quite fulfilled your expectations (true). You've been patient and understanding about the problem (true). Maybe if you privately studied some of those explicit magazines at the bookstore you could pick up some tips or techniques that might help both of you (false).

Suppose you're employed as purchasing manager for a manufacturing plant. A new salesman offers your primary raw product at a discount, but then points out its substandard quality. Unless you're desperate for a short-term savings, you would show your visitor the door. Or picture the same scenario, except that the salesman purposely fails to reveal his product's poor quality. As an astute executive, you instruct your lab to evaluate the material. It dissolves in water like the Wicked Witch of the West in *The Wizard of Oz*. Again, you sweep the salesman out the door.

Now why can't Christian men dispose of Satan and his deceptions so easily? Sometimes Satan is so obvious, like the salesman revealing the poor quality of his material. He practically puts up a billboard: "IF YOU ACCEPT THIS PRIVATE

BUSINESS LUNCHEON WITH THAT WOMAN WHO'S
BEEN FLIRTING WITH YOU, IT WILL LEAD TO A
VERY PLEASURABLE AFFAIR, THOUGH IT MAY
CAUSE SERIOUS COMPLICATIONS LATER." Even
though the cost of doing business with Satan may be fairly up
front at times, our weakness often allows the brightness of the
present to outshine the future. Knowing our lust for present
gratification, Satan uses a preview of coming attractions to
deceive us into taking the wrong path.

Other times, like the deceiving salesman, Satan knows that
he must conceal much more: "What's the harm in accepting an
innocent meeting with a client?" he whispers with the seasoned
voice of reason. "Especially one who obviously appreciates
your keen knowledge of the business?" No billboard warnings
here. Instead, a fat worm on a hook. And once we bite, Satan's
steady hand reels us in.

A DEAL YOU *CAN* REFUSE

A man may acquiesce to an overt temptation, willfully jumping into sin. Or he may become caught in a more covert snare,
where through naïveté or passivity he foolishly subjects himself
to undue temptation. In either case, the common element is
man's ability to be deceived.

But the question remains unanswered: Why can't a Christian man, one with a renewed mind who sincerely wants to
serve God, simply recognize the handiwork of his enemy and
avoid such deception? While being reborn in Christ can be a
dramatic turning point in a person's life, the evidence of
change may come more gradually. Jessie Penn-Lewis offers this
insight in her study of the Ephesians 6:10-17 passage on spiritual warfare: "And the deception of the evil one does not end
when the regenerating life of God reaches the man, for the
blinding of the mind is only removed just so far as the deceptive lies of Satan are dislodged by the light of truth."[2]

Satanic deception is so difficult to recognize because it operates within the principle, or law, of sin. When a man receives salvation, he changes bosses, the Bible says. He becomes a servant of righteousness instead of a servant of sin.

One problem, though. His rebirth does not *erase* the law of sin from the spiritual physics textbook, any more than an airplane flight nullifies the law of gravity. Any man who has struggled with ever-present, powerful urges—such as greed, lust for power, selfishness, or sexual appetite—can identify with the apostle Paul's discourse about this stubborn law of sin, which is part and parcel of being a human being:

> I know that nothing good lives in me, that is, in my sinful nature. For I have the desire to do what is good, but I cannot carry it out. For what I do is not the good I want to do; no, the evil I do not want to do—this I keep on doing. Now if I do what I do not want to do, it is no longer I who do it, but it is sin living in me that does it.
>
> So I find this law at work: When I want to do good, evil is right there with me. For in my inner being I delight in God's law; but I see another law at work in the members of my body, waging war against the law of my mind and making me a prisoner of the law of sin at work within my members. **Romans 7:18-23**

The seed of God's life takes root and grows in a carnal creature used to obeying the law of sin. This internal contradiction explains why fine Christian men can succumb to the worst of temptations, and some of the most stupid ones at that. Whether Satan dons his best disguise or comes at us with his cards on the table, he finds something in man quite willing to be deceived.

Many of us find this basic weakness a hard pill to swallow. Being the self-sufficient creatures we are, we struggle to climb whatever ladder we've chosen, employ our soundest reason, and fight to build a good reputation. We balk at the thought that not only are we rotten to the core, but we're practically blind to the extent of the internal rot. Look again at Penn-Lewis' insight into deception: "Deceived! How the word repels, and how involuntarily every human being resents it as applied to himself, not knowing that the very repulsion is the work of the deceiver for the purpose of keeping the deceived ones from knowing the truth, and being set free from deception."[3]

Our soft underbelly of self-deception, rooted in the law of sin, supplies a crucial piece of information in spiritual warfare. Satan already knows your vulnerability. You need to make some personal discovery of how that frailty affects you, just as the apostle Paul found this law of sin to be a work in his own members. No man should forget his vulnerability if he expects to be an effective warrior.

Time and spiritual maturity serve only to increase the danger for some. Recent scandals involving several Evangelical leaders demonstrate how gifted and apparently godly men can allow the law of sin to shred their ministries and ruin their lives. Whether the lure is money, power, or sex, we would all do well to remember God's word through the prophet Jeremiah: "The heart is deceitful above all things and beyond cure. Who can understand it?" (Jeremiah 17:9).

TEMPTATION AND TRIAL

We often consider temptation as quite separate and distinct from deception. Temptation is nothing more, however, than a manifestation of the deceiver's nature. Every temptation from Satan is essentially a business proposition: you get something, but it costs you. We always find deception entwined in the promised reward as well: what you get never equals the price.

One axiom of economics is that a present dollar is worth more than a future dollar. Satan, likewise, plays upon the high value we place on the present. The discrepancy between what temptation promises and what we pay for giving in is often a matter of time. We may use a half-truth at work to cover up a mistake, but suffer serious disciplinary measures later when the full truth comes to light. We may fudge on our taxes now, but be indicted for tax evasion down the road. We may indulge in illicit sexual pleasure now, but pay the price of months of marital conflict and counseling later on. We may enjoy alcohol-induced merriment now, but fight against alcoholism for years to come. The well-known words of Romans 6:23 summarize the ultimate penalty: "For the wages of sin is death."

Temptation has another sense. James 1:2 tells us, "Consider it pure joy, my brothers, whenever you face trials of many kinds." If you read this same passage in the King James Bible, "trials" is rendered "temptations." Both translations are correct. The relationship shows up more clearly later in the chapter when we see how "trial," "test," and "tempt" are used together: "Blessed is the man who perseveres under trial, because when he has stood the test, he will receive the crown of life that God has promised to those who love him. When tempted, no one should say, 'God is tempting me.' For God cannot be tempted by evil, nor does he tempt anyone" (James 1:12-13).

A trial from God is a test or exercise in faith. A trial from Satan is a temptation to do evil. While they have utterly opposing purposes, both trials can be compared to a pregnancy test: they prove what's inside. Or to put it another way, they push the pedal to the mettle.

Consider how God tested his chosen servant Abraham, whose name meant "father of a multitude." He was asked to believe that God would send him and Sarah a son as they approached their one-hundredth birthdays—no small test, mind you. Abraham eventually panicked and conceived a son named Ishmael with Sarah's serving girl (albeit at his wife's suggestion). In typical male fashion, he rationalized that this avenue of action would allow God to fulfill his promise. Finally the promised son came through Sarah's miraculous pregnancy.

God raised the stakes in the next test when he told Abraham to sacrifice Isaac on a mountain top. No doubt this blew a fuse in the circuitry of the patriarch's brain. If God had told him to stretch his faith for a promised son, and the son had come in an obviously miraculous fashion, then certainly Isaac was the handiwork of God. Why would this same God now command him to kill the boy?

Abraham was experiencing a trial, a testing. I imagine Satan was at work, too, tempting Abraham to ignore God, to disobey God, to get angry and pout at God. How this man of faith handled the situation revealed what was deep inside. The patriarch obeyed God and raised his knife to slay his only beloved son. Convinced of his obedience, God sent an angel to reverse the execution order at the last moment. Scripture tells us repeatedly that Abraham's faith was reckoned to him as righteousness. He passed the test.

SATAN'S KIND OF TEST

As James explains, God tries us so that we can pass the test and receive his approval. God cannot be tempted toward evil, and he never lures his people into evil. Satan, on the other hand, does tempt us to do evil. His efforts surface in three basic ways:

The world. After Jesus had been weakened by his forty days in the desert, Satan offered him all the world's kingdoms. The power, splendor, and wealth of the world never cease to attract men throughout their lives.

The flesh. The flesh involves more than just the obvious carnalities of excessive eating or illicit sex. How about our habits and secret loves—like the temper unleashed on defenseless family members, the fanciful flights of prideful thought, or the insistence upon Sunday afternoons spent watching football on television—that we refuse to relinquish?

The devil. The world and the flesh provide an unending source of temptation, more than enough to cause a man to descend into utter spiritual filth. Yet Satan is not above putting some icing on this mud pie. He especially targets those who, through godly discipline and the strength of the Holy Spirit, have begun to recognize and resist the deceptive lures of the world and the flesh.

You may well ponder why your four-year-old son suddenly hauls off and slugs his two-year-old sister without any provocation. Children need to be trained in everything except sin. The same holds true for adults. Even though they may have received fine spiritual training, grown men will find that Satan can help to generate some unusually base and creative promptings to do all kinds of evil.

The world, the flesh, and the devil represent the nitty-gritty of Satan's mode of operation, where bayonet meets bayonet on the battlefield of spiritual warfare. The man who is unprepared for Satan's attacks faces the likelihood of a spiritually fatal injury. James 1:14-15 summarizes the deadly process: "Each one is tempted when, by his own evil desire, he is dragged away and enticed. Then, after desire has conceived, it gives birth to sin; and sin, when it is full-grown, gives birth to death." But for the man who chooses against the evil brought by Satan, who endures the test brought by God, "he will receive the crown of life that God has promised to those who love him" (James 1:12).

ACCUSER

The Hebrew word translated as Satan means attacker or accuser. As the Bible draws to a close, a reference to Satan emphasizes this particular side of his nature: "For the accuser of our brothers, who accuses them before our God day and night, has been hurled down" (Revelation 12:10). If Satan is accusing us day and night, then we're subject to a torrent of blame. How do we respond to this primary tactic of our enemy?

One way is to defend ourselves, which we sometimes try to do with gusto. But we really don't need to defend ourselves against charges emanating from the "father of lies." If the accusations are false, you should brush them off like flies at a picnic. If they're true—shining a spotlight on one of your sins—defending yourself will not work.

The second response remedies the impasse. Hidden in Christ, we can rebuke Satan from the moral high ground of forgiveness. Yes, we have sinned. Yes, we are guilty. But we no longer need to tote the heavy backpack of condemnation. Of course, to make this declaration, we must first repent of the sin and ask God's forgiveness.

Caught up in the smoke and dust and noise and confusion of an intense battle, modern-day troops have reported that they don't always know where the bullets are coming from or where theirs are going. As a result, soldiers have been killed by "friendly fire," shots delivered by their own side.

In the heat of the spiritual struggles that mark daily life, getting an accurate read on your conscience can be equally tricky, as dangerous as friendly fire. Is that blip on your moral radar the hint of an incoming message from God about some area of sin? Or is Satan throwing darts at you again?

If it's conviction from God, one single act of genuine repentance brings peace. First John 1:9 promises, "If we confess our sins, he is faithful and just and will forgive us our sins and purify us from all unrighteousness." Purification leaves no trace of volatile dirt to fuel the fires of condemnation. If it's Satan, no number of repentances and no amount of deal-making will result in an awareness of purification. Instead, we're left with a lingering sense of unworthiness in the form of unanswered accusations and an unshakable feeling of failure.

Satan often succeeds by blurring the line between temptation and sin. Suppose you've begun to resent your neighbor, an extrovert who's fond of throwing raucous backyard parties and who has expressed amoral opinions you wouldn't even expect to hear from a radical college student. Normal repulsion shouldn't be confused with sin. Yet you need to be aware of the *opportunity* to sin. If you nurture those personal differences and petty offenses into hatred, utilizing every chance to speak evil of your neighbor and secretly wishing the worst disasters would befall him, you have fallen into temptation and are sinning. You have disobeyed Hebrews 12:15: "See to it... that no bitter root grows up to cause trouble...."

A problem person always presents you with an opportunity to dig deep and allow the life of Christ to shine forth in you. Pray for whatever that annoying person may need—salvation, humbling, spiritual reawakening, true friendship, for example. Think love. You don't have to speak approvingly, but you can speak lovingly when you see someone whom you find repulsive. Act with love, even when your efforts are not reciprocated. But above all, recognize your initial reaction for what it is and do not accept Satan's indictment of sin.

Satan always stands ready to fling bogus accusations our way. He loves to exaggerate our weaknesses into overwhelming obstacles, even though they may not be sinful. Failing to recognize and deal properly with his accusations can be particularly discouraging to a man. Because our male nature tends to seek visible accomplishment, to obtain and use power in the establishment of an identity, Satan's accusations can emasculate us swifter than a well-aimed machete:

- "It took you quite a while before you realized you were lusting after that woman starring in the movie last night. And you think you're qualified to lead the prayer session with the singles group at church?"

- "You missed your daughter's last two ballet recitals. She can see you for the kind of father you really are. Do you really think she'll accept your discipline with any authority?"

- "That's the third rebuke from your supervisor this week. And you let your temper flare up again by dishing it right back. You're never going anywhere in your career. You might as well go back to school."

If Satan continues to harass you, fight back with the sharp sword of the Word of God. A good all-purpose Scripture against accusation and condemnation is Romans 8:1-2: "Therefore, there is now no condemnation for those who are in Christ Jesus, because through Christ Jesus the law of the spirit of life set me free from the law of sin and death."

God promises life, not death, as our inheritance in Christ. No amount of sin, no number of repeated failures in a certain weakness, no evidence, however glaring, that the law of sin still operates in your life, can force you to accept condemnation. Christ's death paid the price for your sins. And the Holy Spirit dwells within your heart to set you free from the slavery to sin, a bondage that you could not break with your own power.

Power permeates God's Word. You need to have it in your arsenal to successfully duel with your powerful enemy. If you have trouble memorizing Scripture, do the best you can with a paraphrase (and keep trying to memorize, even if it's just a phrase). If you're able to say it out loud, so much the better; if not, the authority of God's Word still works. The outcome of our battle against the accuser is clear: "They overcame him by the blood of the Lamb [Christ] and by the word of their testimony..." (Revelation 12:11).

RESISTING THE DESTROYER

Beware the tendency to reduce spiritual warfare to little more than a clever metaphor expressing the age-old struggle between good and evil. The battle is deadly serious. Carefully consider one final aspect of Satan's nature: he destroys, he devours, he kills. If he can't kill you spiritually—by destroying or preventing your salvation—he's not above messing around with your body.

In a messianic reference, Satan is pictured as a dragon who "stood in front of the woman who was about to give birth, so that he might devour her child the moment it was born"

(Revelation 12:4). You can be sure that the devil harbors the same kind of harmful intentions for those who follow that child. Satan wants to destroy the life of Christ that keeps multiplying every time a sinner repents and dies to his old life, allowing the new life to begin filling him.

Perhaps more than the other disciples, Peter vividly experienced just how deceptive Satan can be. Desperately wanting to destroy Peter's mighty ministry before it got started, the enemy attempted to cripple this apostle's faith. When Peter rebuked his Master for prophesying his own suffering and death, Jesus delivered a stinging rebuke to a spiritually blind follower: "Get behind me, Satan! You are a stumbling block to me; you do not have in mind the things of God, but the things of men" (Matthew 16:23). When the Lord walked on the water, Peter was eager to do the same, except that he began to sink when his faith weakened. As the crucifixion approached, Peter swore that he would never deny Jesus, but he did three times.

As Peter blazed a trail for the gospel after Jesus' resurrection, he gradually gained a more realistic perspective on himself and Satan. This apostle describes the spiritual enemy who is out to destroy us and offers a sober warning: "Be self-controlled and alert. Your enemy the devil prowls around like a roaring lion looking for someone to devour. Resist him, standing firm in the faith" (1 Peter 5:8-9). This passage offers three helpful pointers:

Be self-controlled. The soldier in control of himself focuses on his officer's orders and the mission at hand. He will not let other people or circumstances dictate what he does. Early in Saul's reign as king over Israel, he received instructions from the prophet Samuel: attack the Amalekites and kill all the people and animals. Saul cinched the victory, but lost control of himself. He spared the Amalekite king, Agag, along with all the choice sheep and cattle. Saul's lame excuse? He wanted to offer the livestock as an offering to the Lord. After Samuel's rebuke, Saul admitted that he had taken his eyes off his orders: "I was afraid of the people and so I gave in to them" (1 Samuel 15:24).

When they are insecure in their identity, most men fear what people think of them. They tend to do foolish things in their miscalculated attempts to retain a position of leadership. Satan exploited Saul's loss of self-control through an act of disobedience which sealed the destruction of his kingship. Samuel spoke the final judgment: "The Lord has rejected you as king over Israel" (1 Samuel 15:26).

Be alert. Scripture describes Satan as a prowling lion looking for someone to devour. The imagery is terrifyingly accurate. We may entertain sin for weeks, months, years, never aware of the lion who stalks us. When we do hear an occasional roar, we rationalize that it must be meant for someone else.

When a real lion decides he's close enough to sprint in for the kill, his prey cannot mount the running start necessary to escape slaughter. We can be trapped in the same way whenever festering, secret sin is exposed and all the consequences come crashing down. How many marriages have been plunged into a hopeless spiral of destruction because a husband refused to be alert to his prowling enemy, allowing himself to fall victim to ever-increasing abuse of alcohol, all the while denying his sickness?

Resist him, standing firm in the faith. A man in control of himself, alert at all times, has already begun to resist the enemy. He has removed the important element of surprise which is so crucial to Satan, who is much weaker than God and who depends so much on deception. Such a man can stand firm with faith as his greatest defensive weapon, a shield "with which you can extinguish all the flaming arrows of the evil one" (Ephesians 6:16).

When Satan faces a self-controlled, alert man, ordinary temptations of the world and the flesh may prove fruitless. Even so, Satan can usually find a few crevices into which his thin poison can seep. One such deadly toxin is doubt. No man is perfectly confident about every aspect of his relationship with God. Satan enjoys poking around to find those crevices, whether they be major theological issues or seemingly trivial incidents. Am I really saved? If Christianity is true, why is there so much denominational division? If God hears prayers, why doesn't he answer me more often? Why am I suffering financially when I'm doing everything I know possible to please God? How could my pastor have made that snide remark to me and at the same time be a man of God?

These and countless other speculations lead to discouragement, doubt, and defeat. James advises the man of God not only to resist, but to do so *firm* in the faith. Whatever measure of faith God has given you at this stage in your life, pull it tight when the time for conflict arises, just as a runner tightens his shoelaces in preparation for a race. Fall back on Scripture as non-negotiable truth. Recall the good things that God has already done in your life beyond any shadow of doubt.

Now that we've taken a closer look at our Enemy, let's consider the warriors whom he faces. Do we truly know our own strengths and weaknesses?

THREE

Portrait of the Male Warrior

W HEN ASKED BY A MINISTER to name the central focus in his family life, a teenage boy quickly responded, "The TV."

"What's next?"

"The cat," said the youth.

The minister tried a different tack: Which person was the focal point of the household?

"My mother."

What about his father? What did the son observe the father doing?

"Eating, watching television, and sleeping," he responded.

Hardly criminal activities, but if that's the dominant impression a father leaves on his children, then he's sitting on a tall stack of past-due bills for responsibility and leadership. God expects much more, and not just from fathers and husbands. Without family responsibilities and the companionship of a wife, single men can feel they *deserve* to fill those long, lonely hours at home with diversions such as food, TV, and sleep, sometimes in massive quantities.

The uniqueness of the male blueprint affects not only the way Satan can attack men but also the way we can enter into battle. Men often succeed or fail as spiritual warriors because of common physical and psychological qualities. Having studied male weaknesses since the world began, Satan's got us pegged. If you want to resist him, you need to make sure you understand yourself as well as your enemy does. How vulnerable is the male warrior?

DAY IN AND DAY OUT

A recent survey asked men what they most wanted in their homes: "Men did not long for expensive furniture, well-equipped garages, or a private study in which to work. What they wanted most was *tranquility* at home. Competition is so fierce in the workplace today and the stresses of pleasing a boss and surviving professionally are so severe, that the home needs to be a haven to which a man can return."[1]

I don't disagree that a man's home should be a haven where his favorite recliner does wonders for the back and legs after putting mind and muscles through the wringer all day. But the time away from a job demands much more than simply rest. No matter how vicious a boss or business competitor may be, punching a time card does not equate with pushing a pause button on conflict, spiritual and otherwise.

Why do men sometimes idealize home as a resort at which they are the chief customers? Society tends to measure a man's worth by his success at work. Achievement that can be measured—by sales quotas, titles, promotions, and income—appeals to the male ego. When someone gives himself over completely to that value system, he sees no reason to turn around and make home another production-oriented situation, one that cannot even be measured quantitatively.

A man's drive for success can become a strength rather than a weakness. We need to learn how to shift gears and apply our workplace assets to the spiritual life and family. We need to harness that same drive that helps employees discipline their time and subordinate immature emotions or behaviors. For example, a man will not shirk his scheduled daily time to pray and study the Bible if he truly views it as an engagement with the most important boss in his life—the Lord. By the same token, a committed husband will not cancel an engagement with his wife just to play poker with the guys.

Good Christian soldiers cannot afford to go above and beyond the call of duty at work and then come home feeling depleted for the rest of the job God has given them. Whether it's a father caring for his family, or a single man serving in a soup kitchen, or a mature widower sharing his wisdom through a church class, there are many opportunities to serve outside the workplace.

Satan never takes a weekend off or calls a time-out. The spiritual battle rages on, day in and day out. The question is: Will you fight it? Or will you leave it to someone else—your minister, your wife, or your friend who seems more interested in spiritual affairs? With whatever strength you possess, will you do your part in fighting for the establishment of God's kingdom?

God needs men like the three hundred warriors who followed Gideon. They could have demanded a long lunch break after surprising and routing the Midianites in the middle of the night. Instead, these soldiers found themselves "weary, yet pursuing" the Midianites as the day wore on (Judges 8:4). When Gideon's hungry men paused at Succoth to request bread, the city officials denied them. They made the same request of men at Peniel and were rejected again. But hunger didn't stop Gideon's crew. They surprised the enemy, pursuing and capturing the two kings and routing the entire army. On their return trip, they fulfilled Gideon's promise to those who had refused him help: at Peniel, the Hebrews tore down the tower and killed the male inhabitants; at Succoth, Gideon had the elders flailed with thorns and briers.

God often calls his men to pursue the enemy even when weariness seems to numb every muscle. The viability of family and church depends on strong, productive men, willing to move from one battle front to the next, without adequate rest when necessary. God will supply the strength you need.

WAR-WEARY OR WAR-WISE?

Military forces have traditionally relied on men in part because they can tolerate intense physical hardship—including deprivation of sleep, comfort, and food. The man who is capable of physical and mental discipline should also apply these strengths to his spiritual walk. He can embrace the attitude expressed by Paul: "I beat my body and make it my slave..." (1 Corinthians 9:27).

Endurance and a high tolerance for physical hardship also prove advantageous in spiritual warfare. Real wars don't last an hour. They're rarely won in a matter of days or weeks. Many wars throughout history have dragged on over years, leaving a stinking trail of bloody corpses. In the same way, a spiritual soldier shouldn't sign up expecting to serve as a weekend warrior in the reserve unit. Sometimes God will answer a petition with surprising speed, but more often, it takes longer—days, months, even years—much longer than we, in our limited time frame, consider proper.

Endurance in spiritual warfare often involves more than simply prolonged asking and receiving. In the last few years, I have seen a rash of divorce, separations, and near-separations among Christian couples I know. None of them decided to split up because hubby forgot the anniversary, or because the wife suddenly went on a spending spree. Their problems had been brewing for years, allowing Satan to establish the equivalent of a military stronghold within the marriage.

Where no remarriage has occurred, God can certainly choose to reconcile these couples in some dramatic way. In one case, he simultaneously initiated a surprising change of heart in both partners, even though the healing is far from complete. In any marriage which reaches the point of separation, one has to assume that Satan will not easily forsake his hard-earned stronghold. I continue to pray for many of these embattled couples. Enough sniper fire over a long period can wear down the most entrenched position.

A man's physical strength also comes into play in the discipline of children. While both parents need to contribute, most Christian mothers notice a certain persuasive force resides in a spiritually active, physically strong man that women cannot duplicate. At the simplest level, this is the ability to deliver effective discipline. When my wife becomes frustrated in persuading our younger boys to clean up a messy den, she is quick to brandish the name "Daddy." The threat usually gets results. Sometimes it gets Daddy, and he gets results.

Psycholgical endurance also can be an asset of the male warrior. Because men tend to be task-oriented, they can be masters of the long haul. "Men work real well in military situations because they can fixate," said one pastor. "They don't deviate from the objective." This trait also commonly translates into objectivity. Those men who possess a strongly rational mind can pierce the clouds and winds of subjective emotions. As circumstances change, men are often able to stick with the plan.

Suppose a husband and wife decide their son needs to quit spending time with a neighborhood friend who has proven himself to be a bad influence. As days elapse, the son pouts because his "only friend" is off-limits. The friend makes a point of drifting by the house to talk to the wife, being careful to say "Yes, ma'am," and talking about school projects and team sports. She soon softens: "He really seems to have changed.... Every boy needs a good friend in the neighborhood.... I thought it would be okay to let them spend just an hour or so together, as long as their homework was done."

Granted, part of being an effective leader is knowing when to change your mind—but leadership often means learning *not* to change your mind. An effective father will continue monitoring such a situation, heeding his wife's observations, and taking it before God in prayer. He may end up playing the heavy, deciding to persevere with the original dictum. There's no guarantee that all parties involved will be smiling at this father a week later, or maybe for months. There's no guarantee that he'll be proven right. But the father may be called upon to remember the initial problem and the agreed-upon solution, and then be willing to ride that bronco until it's broken.

A career military man who fought under General George Patton in Europe explained how he could identify a good field officer: one who knew how and when to retreat—and that usually meant as fast as any coward could run. But the good officer also knew how to pursue, and pursue some more, just as General Thomas "Stonewall" Jackson did in the Civil War.

A man's willingness to jump into the fray is particularly helpful in what's known as deliverance ministry—prayer to deliver people from one or more demons that continually oppress them. Complementing this readiness to respond can be a male's capacity for calmness or coolness in battle. One man who specializes in a deliverance ministry noted the male "aspect of courage, a kind of male response to roll your sleeves up, jump into a good fight, and go at it swinging."

While the male warrior's physical strength and psychological endurance can be important assets in battle, he also exhibits certain weaknesses. One key vulnerability stems from a fragile identity, somewhat like a portrait painted with fuzzy outlines. To better understand why a man tends to remain so dependent upon his own imagination and vain constructions, consider some general ways that a male's identity differs from a female's.

THE STRONGER SEX?

A photograph in one of our family albums shows my wife sitting on the couch and cradling our two youngest sons as they guzzled from baby bottles. Cute shot: the contented faces, staring up in unison; an equally contented mother, adoring the two miraculous fruits from her womb. Now imagine Dad inserted in Mom's place. Something gets lost in the translation.

I don't mean to diminish the importance of a father's role, but the totality of maternity seems to carry more tangible weight than paternity. Most women are natural nurturers with a more settled sexual identity.[2] The cycles of menstrual period, pregnancy, lactation, and nursing accentuate the procreative role of females throughout much of their lives.

Men, by contrast, participate in only one act directly related to child-bearing. The survival of the infant doesn't require that the father hang around during the pregnancy, show up at the birth, or stick around thereafter. With artificial insemination becoming more widespread, a woman really doesn't even need a man present to put the baby-making machinery into gear— which suits some feminists just fine.

The sexual identity of the two genders begins to form from birth. A girl naturally bonds with her mother; her sexuality develops in an undisturbed pattern into adolescence and adulthood. A boy also bonds more closely with his mother, but at some early point he begins to dissolve that tie and move into his own male world. Ideally a boy identifies with his father, temporarily relinquishing the kind of intimacy he shared with his mother.

If all goes well, the father models strength, stability, sacrifice, and leadership. And particularly through his demonstration of love, tempered by judgment and mercy, the spiritually mature father reflects the fatherhood of God. A son raised with that kind of influence will be well-equipped to make the transition into independent adulthood and fatherhood. However, fathers are only human, as we all know too well. Every father does less than a perfect job in raising children, whether they be sons or daughters. Each of us exits our formative years with various dints and dings to our exterior finish as well as to our interior machinery.

Finding a suitable mate helps to re-establish that bond of intimacy from childhood. But being a grown-up usually means finding a job before getting married. Yet even having a successful career fails to stabilize a man's fragile sense of identity. What do men ask each other when they meet? The classic probe: *What do you do?* And we all understand "do" to mean paid employment.

Though men don't typically divulge salaries, society defines occupational currency in familiar ways: banker is worth more than carpenter; regional manager ranks above branch manager; white collar bests blue collar. Realizing that many people remain unaware of the jobs they hold, successful men sometimes resort to highly leveraged, passive advertising—notably by driving a sleek car and living in the nicest neighborhood that borrowed money will buy.

The point is not so much to grimace over man's plight, but to understand the male warrior and move on. God did not use the wrong software when he programmed man. Basic masculinity will not change. As members of the human race, we remain weak and vulnerable on many fronts. But God has promised that his strength is made perfect in our weakness (2 Corinthians 12:9).

Living with weakness can be one of the most difficult tasks of all. Man, like nature, abhors a vacuum. He will not hesitate—though perhaps unaware of what he's doing—to fill up any barrenness in his life. Satan is constantly maneuvering to suggest this habit or that diversion as the stuffing for that soul hole. After returning from an international conference of Christian counselors, a pastor noted one consensus among the group: "We're fast becoming a world of addictions." Many addicts are men, struggling with basic insecurity.

Prolonged or seemingly insurmountable failure too often leads to addictions in a person's attempt to compensate. One man invested his identity in his business. As it began to fail, the void in his life grew larger. He poured in alcohol and sexual immorality. Even though a counselor pointed out his downward cycle, this man couldn't break out of it. He eventually left his wife and lost his business.

Being a faithful husband and father requires constant vigilance and spiritual warfare, fighting on the home front for whatever is righteous and life-giving. Every man needs to be walking in a close relationship with God, where his identity as a son of the Father transcends his needs for acceptance and intimacy. If not, he will remain vulnerable to spiritual attack.

A lesson in naked male insecurity. Having begun his reign at age thirty, Saul tended to be impetuous at times. Samuel, the prophet who had anointed him king, called the young king to meet him at Gilgal. Meanwhile, some of the Hebrew soldiers attacked a Philistine outpost, arousing the wrath of the entire enemy army. Knowing Israel was at the top of the Philistine hit list, Saul summoned all his troops to join him at Gilgal. The Hebrews were vastly outnumbered, yet were under orders not to retreat. The Philistines had three thousand chariots; Israel had none. Painfully aware of their predicament, Saul's troops began hiding in caves, thickets, and holes. Some deserted and fled across the Jordan River. Those who remained were "quaking with fear" (1 Samuel 13:7).

Saul waited seven days as Samuel had instructed, but still no prophet. More men began to scatter. As the heat intensified, Saul began to melt. Did he have the strength as a leader to keep the remainder of his army intact? Was the newly appointed king of Israel secure enough as a man of God to continue waiting for Samuel, to trust God's protection if a superior force attacked? Did Saul fear disobeying God more than displeasing his troops? Would he wait for Samuel's arrival before going ahead with the sacrifice, as the prophet had commanded?

No on all counts. Samuel arrived just as Saul finished offering the sacrifice. The king offered the lame excuse that the Philistines were about to attack and he had not yet sought the Lord's favor through a burnt offering. Because of Saul's disobedience and lack of faith, Samuel prophesied that his kingdom would not endure.

While you probably haven't been tested that severely, certain circumstances may have revealed your insecurities, just as Saul's bubbled to the surface under pressure. Most of us have faced workplace situations where we had to perform at a certain standard, and we weren't prepared. Or we've had to muddle through marital conflicts, knowing we were shooting from the hip, not likely to hit the target of a wise resolution.

Even the man who is outwardly the strongest has some points of weakness. And his reluctance to admit them makes him more vulnerable because sooner or later, Samuel will arrive, and with him a day of reckoning. We may repress our weaknesses, but they whisper to us from deep inside. Unless our identities are firmly grounded on the rock of Christ, they will begin to fall apart whenever our fears and weaknesses undermine our confidence. We will discover we are men with feet of clay.

KEEPING THE LINES OF COMMUNICATION OPEN

My boys used to ask me to imitate Porky Pig, the speech-impaired cartoon character. The lisping stutter always got plenty of laughs. While I don't normally stutter, I have noticed some sort of inborn handicap when it comes to expressing myself verbally. I sometimes entertain the private pleasure of just, well, shutting up. Why bother to say any more than you have to, especially to your wife, who's heard it all before anyway? Why recount a blow-by-blow description of some trivial conversation with someone when a short and sweet summary will suffice?

Why, indeed? Some men are fairly verbal, though this is known to be women's strong suit. But another communication deficit strikes me as even more profound: *confession*. By this I mean two things. One is saying something that's awkward, even embarrassing, such as apologizing to your four-year-old for losing your temper after he used a rock to scratch on the hood of your new car. The other aspect of confession involves the internal process of admitting something that's difficult, such as confessing to the Lord that yes, you do resent your neighbor because his wife makes all that money as a lawyer and one family doesn't really deserve that much income.

Why this aversion to admitting our weaknesses? Male vulnerability places too much at stake. If a man builds his identity as a shrewd businessman, the slightest sign of a professional mistake or failure becomes magnified in his eyes. (You can also count on Satan to be handy with a high-powered microscope.) When someone envisions himself to be a prototype family man, disaffection from his wife or unruliness from his children may embarrass him to the point of utter shame. Admitting a major failure can be tantamount to psychological suicide— killing off your own identity when you become something less than what you wanted others to think you were.

There is nothing magical about confession. Then why does it often prove to be such a dramatic step forward in counseling or in a man's relationship to God? Simply because confession is a declaration of truth. No more hiding behind phony smiles, empty rituals, or meaningless promises.

Scripture describes the battle which we fight as one which pits light against darkness: "Everyone who does evil hates the light, and will not come into the light for fear that his deeds will be exposed. But whoever lives by the truth comes into the light, so that it may be seen plainly that what he has done has been done through God" (John 3:20-21). The essence of truth and light are found in Jesus, who identified himself as the way, the truth, and the life (John 14:6), as well as the light: "I am the light of the world. Whoever follows me will never walk in darkness, but will have the light of life" (John 8:12).

How does one live by the truth, and thereby stay in this floodlight that flushes out the shadows? We should confess our sins, our fears, our deepest inadequacies to God. First John 1:9 instructs: "If we confess our sins, he is faithful and just and will forgive us our sins and purify us from all unrighteousness." Scripture promises not just forgiveness, and with it the removal of guilt, but purification as well. The addictions, the habits, the idols that fill our lives can be partially, if not fully, driven out through the confession of sin and ongoing repentance.

As a man becomes grounded in unconditional acceptance by God and those around him, he begins to form an identity that doesn't hinge on job, wealth, or the approval of other men or his wife. He need not compensate for his failures through euphoric escapes into alcohol or drugs or the passing pleasures of illicit sex. A healthy self-image need not be replaced with the puffery of worldly power.

Only in Jesus, as our elder brother, do we find a clear path to the heavenly Father, the one whose unconditional love upholds us. And through Jesus, we have the privilege of standing before the Father faultless upon confession of our sins. Therein lies true acceptance, true sonship. We in no way have earned or deserve such a relationship; it is granted as a gift. God only asks that we love him in return with a whole heart.

DISCOVERING THE SPIRITUAL DIMENSION

Do you ever feel like you've got a little cotton in your spiritual ears? Too many men are more interested in tangible production or physical things than intangible prayer or spiritual matters. Sure, we'll serve God through the church. Put us on the finance committee, the site-search committee, the building committee. Don't hesitate to call. But the weekly morning prayer meeting? Don't bother to call. It's so hard to *find time,* you see. And besides, the women seem to handle the praying end of things so well.

"Women are more eager to be involved in spiritual things," confirmed one man in full-time ministry. "I guess men tend toward the tangibles, project orientation, what-are-we-going-to-do kinds of things—whether working with numbers, facilities, or projects—and so deeper spirituality is more elusive."

Many women find deep fulfillment in building relationships; many men would just as soon build cars. Or computers or roads. Or factories, so they can build even more things. The idea of investing an hour a week in group prayer, or fifteen minutes a day in personal prayer, for weeks, months, who knows how long, and getting uncertain results, or perhaps no tangible results at all, does not compute with a man's definition of a fruitful investment. Our linear mind looks down the end of the production line and expects something that, by a certain date, can be seen and touched. With strengths in rational, linear thought, many men are good with numbers and can easily visualize in three dimensions. That's why we often make proficient architects and engineers.

Yet when it comes to spiritual matters, we tend to be less than adept. Lacking a strong intuitive sense, we often flounder, looking for a way to plug in to the unseen realm. Take prayer, for example. To become more interesting than a Christmas wish-list of desired healings and blessings, prayer must reach the level of a conversation. You speak, God speaks, you speak, God speaks, and so on. No man is so superficial, so un-intuitive, that he cannot gradually build a warm communion with his heavenly Father. But doing so requires time and commitment, just as any friendship does. The encouraging part is that God is eager to reciprocate in the relationship.

Spiritual sensitivity also comes into play in other facets of spiritual warfare. As later chapters will discuss, certain occasions benefit from discernment. This is the ability to sense a particular presence or strategy of Satan—say, a nagging sin problem that a person cannot shake, even with repentance.

God never expects you to survive enemy attacks by relying solely on your natural strengths. His armory includes six critical pieces of equipment at our disposal to combat our deceptive, accusing, and destructive enemy. The next chapter will show what defensive and offensive power this battle gear provides.

FOUR

Your Battle Gear

B ECAUSE WE HAD NO DAUGHTERS, I assumed that my wife and I would escape clothes crises as we marched through the valley of the shadow of parenthood. I was wrong. Which shoes or clothes are to be worn by certain sons has become the most regular topic of what could politely be called family discussions.

While the issue of clothing seems so superficial, it hangs on something a little deeper than what is only skin-deep. Brands, colors, loose-or-tight fit—such trivial factors are all that stand between a boy's nakedness and an often hostile world. Venturing into school, he subjects himself to insults, comparisons, mild physical attacks, and the tyranny of a fashion status quo that can change more quickly than the lunar cycle. A boy eventually learns that appearance alone cannot guarantee the basic peer acceptance he so desperately seeks. Until he does, his garb provides a head start, a foundation, a defensive measure.

The whims of fashion pander not only to children. The serious careerist can learn how to choose killer clothes or power ties, fashion statements which can help a businessman establish his assertiveness and whack his way through the corporate jungle. In fact, you can even hire full-time consultants who help you shop for the right clothes to fit your career—armor, if you will, in the civilized warfare of modern society.

The apostle Paul understood the importance of armor.

Having been holed up in a Roman prison and then placed under house arrest and chained to a Roman soldier, he used the analogy of a soldier's complete battle outfit to illustrate the preparation of the Christian warrior. In this chapter, we'll look at how God wants to equip every spiritual warrior.

OUR VULNERABILITY

Have you heard the one about why the school bus driver was so carefree? His troubles were all behind him.

Well, unlike that driver, your troubles surround you. You don't have to wait for conflict. At home, on the way to work, at work, at play, at any time, spiritual warfare swirls around you. Minding your own business at home, a co-worker calls on the phone. As the conversation drifts to another employee, you remember a fresh piece of gossip about this person. Since suppressing the juicy tidbit is harder than keeping an inflated tire tube under water, you let it out. After hanging up, you blast your youngest child for pestering you while you were on the phone. Then you resume watching television, only to find a bedroom scene pulling your mind into moral quicksand. Fifteen minutes have passed, and you're zero for three.

Spiritual armor and weapons are not optional. You need to be comfortable with your battle gear and wear it all the time, not just suit up when an attack intensifies. Being properly prepared merely allows you to show up on the battlefield each morning and still be breathing by lunchtime. More experienced spiritual warriors don't receive more advanced weaponry, but the same essentials, whose use is increasingly perfected through serving Christ. Ephesians 6 describes the basic gear necessary for spiritual conflict:

Finally, be strong in the Lord and in his mighty power. Put on the full armor of God so that you can take your stand against the devil's schemes. For our struggle is not against flesh and blood, but against the rulers, against the authorities, against the powers of this dark world and against the spiritual forces of evil in the heavenly realms. Therefore put on the full armor of God, so that when the day of evil comes, you may be able to stand your ground, and after you have done everything, to stand. Stand firm then, with the belt of truth buckled around your waist, with the breastplate of righteousness in place, and with your feet fitted with the readiness that comes from the gospel of peace. In addition to all this, take up the shield of faith, with which you can extinguish all the flaming arrows of the evil one. Take the helmet of salvation and the sword of the Spirit, which is the word of God.   **Ephesians 6:10-17**

Paul makes clear that our fight is not really against the bad guys, or the bad circumstances that we can see and touch. It transpires on an invisible plane. The real enemies are fallen angels—Satan and his demons. Yet he also assures us that our struggle against Satan is not so spooky and overwhelming that we need to shy away from it, leaving it in the hands of full-time Christian professionals. Twice he tells the believers in Ephesus to "put on the full armor of God." We are called to take the initiative.

We are also instructed to "be strong in the Lord and in his mighty power." The Christian warrior is never an independent mercenary, self-trained, self-armed, able to do all things because of singular skill and self-discipline. Rather, he is enlisted in a worldwide army, constantly dependent on God's provision of armor and power. Let's first examine our defensive battle gear piece by piece.

BELT OF TRUTH

Many large businesses develop a formal mission statement, usually a few sentences that explain in a broad way what they hope to accomplish and who they hope will benefit. Avon, for example, states its mission in this way: "To deliver quality products and services, defect-free, on time, at the lowest cost to our representatives, customers, and each other." Sticking to these goals has enabled Avon to stay in business for more than one hundred years and become the world's largest cosmetics company.

Suppose an apparel company defines its mission as delivering quality goods to consumers at a cost low enough to reach a mass market. Such a company probably should refuse an opportunity to acquire a small maker of upscale clothes. Trying to expand its objectives beyond the original scope could well dilute the company's identity and effectiveness, spelling the beginning of the end.

The mission statement, then, serves as a touchstone by which a company can test any decision or opportunity that arises, like whether to relocate, refinance bonds, or change suppliers. If adhered to, this statement will help management hold the loose ends together, reject what is superfluous, and concentrate on what's important. Some matters might be debatable, but the mission statement shines a spotlight of objective truth upon any issue in question.

Paul spoke of a similar tool when he used the image of a "belt of truth." A warrior's belt was wide—more like a girdle than the modern belt—and made of leather. It kept a soldier's armor snug against his body, ensuring that he wouldn't be impeded when marching or fighting. The belt also supported a heavy sword and carried valuables such as money.

In using this imagery, Paul may have been drawing upon Old Testament Scripture that prophesied the coming of Messiah, one who would have righteousness for a belt and faithfulness for a sash (Isaiah 11:5). As the Word of God made flesh, Jesus Christ embodied truth.

The very life of Christ lives in you, as well as the convictions that spring from his life and the revealed Word of his Father. These spiritual realities form the belt of truth that wraps around your life and guards your stance in every area—such as your integrity on the job, your exposure to modern media, your relationships to family and friends. You can weigh every questionable situation, every relationship, every temptation against the mission statement of God's truth as revealed in his Word.

Since the Greek does not say "the truth," some commentators believe that Paul may have been referring not to doctrinal truth but to truth of character, such as sincerity or integrity.[1] This interpretation also goes hand in hand with the undergirding we need as spiritual warriors. A foundation of doctrinal truth should lead to an appropriate expression of character.

The soldier's belt was crucial to his entire outfit. It enabled the warrior to keep a tight ship, to make sure that his armor didn't become so loose that maneuvering became difficult or that arrows or sword points could penetrate the gaps. Consider what happened when King Ahab, one of the most wicked kings of Israel, went into battle. The enemy king had told his thirty-two chariot commanders not to waste time on lower-ranking fighters in the midst of battle, but to look only for the king.

Ahab knew he was a marked man. True to his deceptive nature, he decided to disguise himself. Clever, though not clever enough. It so happened that he was wanted not only by the king of Aram, but by the King of heaven and earth: "But someone drew his bow at random and hit the king of Israel between the sections of his armor.... The blood from his wound ran onto the floor of the chariot, and that evening he died" (1 Kings 22:34-35).

Armor never guarantees survival in spiritual warfare. The enemy will inevitably spot chinks and cracks. And that vulnerability grows if the armor is loose. By keeping the belt of truth tightly buckled, we increase our odds immensely.

BREASTPLATE OF RIGHTEOUSNESS

"Righteousness" refers to your standing before God. When you sin, you are guilty and deserve punishment. Yet because

Christ died for your sins, if you repent of them, you receive a clean slate. The righteousness of Christ, not the tarnished virtue of a sinner, covers your front like a breastplate.

So far, so good. You run into trouble, however, when your breastplate shifts around, exposing a little soft underbelly here, a little rib cage there. Satan and his legions, like the forces of the king of Aram, will be close at hand, spraying you with projectiles, hoping for just one direct hit:

- "You sure lost your temper with that customer on the phone. You're not worthy to hold your job. What about that 'Christian witness' at work you're always talking about?"

- "That was a clever fudge on your part when you returned that appliance for a refund. If you can exaggerate like that for a $49.95 tool, you'll lie about anything. You're a complete moral failure."

- "Your wife sure wanted to have family devotions last night before you ran off to play softball. Looks like you made your priorities clear enough to her. You'll never be the kind of spiritual leader she needs."

The truth can set you free from this barrage of condemnation—the enemy's usual mixture of truth and lies, or an embellishment of your sins and shortcomings. Sure, you regularly fail at home and on the job. But you don't need to reach any set measure of success in either area to prove your manhood. Instead, you are complete in Christ (Colossians 2:10). Your sins are forgiven and you are being progressively sanctified. You are a slave to righteousness (Romans 6:16). Because Jesus took our sin upon himself, we have become the righteousness of God (2 Corinthians 5:21).

Keeping your breastplate secure won't prevent Satan from attacking, but it will enable you to withstand the assault. You can forget to buckle on the truth, go into battle with a loose breastplate, and end up wallowing in your blood, like Ahab. Or you can keep your belt tight and your breastplate in place, and live to fight another day.

THE SHOES OF READINESS

The third piece of battle gear is intended for a less vital part of the male anatomy: "feet fitted with the readiness that comes from the gospel of peace." Paul is referring to the footgear typically worn for long marches. It gave the soldier a solid stance, prevented his feet from sliding, and made him as ready as he could be for any activity.

Wearing any type of footwear was itself an indication of readiness. For instance, when God commanded the Hebrew slaves in Egypt to eat the Passover meal, he instructed them to do so with their sandals on. They needed to be ready to leave for the Promised Land. Readiness also implies keeping one's priorities straight. For example, some physicians carry electronic beepers during their off hours, an indication that their patients can take precedence over activities most of us covet with bared teeth and a low growl, such as sleeping, eating, and recreation.

Spiritual readiness means keeping your ears tuned for a leading from God while living according to his sense of priorities. By presenting himself as ready at all times for service, the spiritual warrior embraces the teaching of 2 Timothy 2:3-4: "Endure hardship with us like a good soldier of Christ Jesus. No one serving as a soldier gets involved in civilian affairs—he wants to please his commanding officer."

A good soldier of Christ Jesus should especially be ready to spread the "gospel of peace" whenever the opportunity arises. Evangelism entails going head-to-head against Satan. While you may not feel especially gifted as an evangelist, you should "be prepared in season and out of season" (2 Timothy 4:2) to articulate the best news anyone will ever hear.

What does the "gospel of peace" bring to mind? Foremost, the sinful creature can be reconciled to the Creator. Once we accept the reality of Jesus' death and resurrection, this *vertical* reunion is relatively easy to swallow. *Horizontal* peace-making between creature and creature tends to be much more difficult. Unresolved hurt feelings, heated disagreements, petty doctrinal differences—these are the sorts of areas Satan uses to sabotage the stability and growth of God's kingdom.

The readiness to be a peacemaker is a crucial part of your spiritual armor. If your feet are shod with the boots of peace, then you're ready to go out and do something with the good news of Jesus Christ. Here are three ways you can march forth to share the gospel with others.

1. Be an effective witness of Christ in word and in deed. I don't mean systematically converting everyone you know, one by one, as if you were shooting down fighter jets in a video game. I mean being honest about why you are the way you are, why you act and talk differently.

John White, in his book *The Fight*, uses the example of laughing at a dirty joke to fit in with the guys at work. Admittedly, some off-color jokes contain humor, but is that the real reason you laugh? Or do you seek the approval of others whose philosophy of life opposes Christ? White recommends: "If some response is demanded, try, 'Look I don't want to embarrass you. I think sex is great. But it's kind of important to me. Maybe too important to joke about lightly.' Your rejoinder, if it is an honest one, may pave the way to a conversation with a more serious tone."[2] The real meaning of being a witness, White goes on to say, is to be a signpost, pointing people to the one who makes you what you are. You want to steer those who are still torn by guilt and frustration toward the true source of peace.

2. Seek peace by minimizing interpersonal conflict within your circle of influence, which includes your friends, your

church, and your family. A woman I know says that her husband is quick to stop her whenever she introduces a topic of concern about a third party if it sounds the least bit suspicious. "Wait a minute. Is this something I really need to know about this person?" he'll ask. His question is no small act of self-discipline. It's much easier—and a lot more fun—to hear the sordid details, then gravely pronounce that you shouldn't have been subjected to such vile gossip. You can even figure out a kosher excuse, usually that so-and-so needs prayer, to repeat the same gossip to someone else.

3. If you're married, your role description calls for a degree of peacemaking that exceeds that of your wife's. In Ephesians 5, the husband is commanded to love his wife, to care for her in the same way that he would care for his own body. Obedience to this command inevitably means sacrificing his time or convenience when his wife has an immediate need. The husband's position as "head of the wife" (Ephesians 5:23) establishes his authority. Because the head generally has a better perspective of how to minimize stress on the body, it also means that he needs to be the first to act whenever conflicts arise.

A husband needs to pull on his gospel boots of peace and keep them laced tight. That can be easier said than done. For example, counselors say that hedging on the part of both partners is a common roadblock in marital success: "I'll start showing more interest in his job if he'll be nicer to me around the children." "I'd be willing to open up more to her if she would quit nagging me about my smoking." Well, this mule ain't leaving the stall. Because no partner is perfect, predicating one's own change on the other person's actions proves to be a recipe for stagnation. And a stagnant marriage, like stagnant water, quickly becomes contaminated.

Whatever spiritual giftings may be evident in your life, you can be certain that God has given you the ministry of reconciliation (2 Corinthians 5:18). God has issued you boots in just the right size. Put them on. Step out. Bring peace!

FROM A TINY FLAME

In addition to the belt of truth, the breastplate of righteousness, and the shoes of the gospel of peace, Paul instructs us to "take up the shield of faith, with which you can extinguish all the flaming arrows of the evil one" (Ephesians 6:16). What are these "flaming arrows" that need to be extinguished? Are they big or small? Are they strong temptations, or merely minor irritations, like being stuck in an interminable summer afternoon rush hour without air conditioning? The arrows can take many different forms:

- You're scheduled to present a new project proposal to all of the department heads. The thought pops into your head that you'd look mighty creative if you neglected to name the person who actually generated the idea. And no one would ever know but you.

- The driver in front of you on the interstate changes lanes so fast that you hit your brakes and swerve, missing an accident by inches. What more justifiable reason could you find to unleash a string of sizzling obscenities that would melt the plastic on your dashboard? The flaming arrows of anger and cursing have hit their mark.

- Your company just announced that it will trim its work force by fifteen percent over the next year. No pink slips have been issued yet, but you know your middle-management position could be very subject to belt-tightening. You have a mortgage, children, debts, and a comfortable life. Finding another job would be difficult, most likely forcing your family to move and make do with a smaller income. You lie awake at night mentally rehearsing all the grim scenarios. A knot grips your stomach most of the day. You're short with your wife and children, angry that they don't seem to understand the pressure you're under.

Fear, temptations, doubts about God, false or exaggerated accusations—such are the sharp-headed missiles that can easily pierce your flesh if you fail to protect yourself. Hoist the shield of faith, advised the apostle Paul. He alluded to the heavy Roman shield made of two layers of wood and bound with iron, large enough to guard the entire body. No self-respecting Roman soldier would ever leave home without it.

This heavy-duty shield was designed with one additional feature: a leather covering. After being soaked in water, the shield could extinguish enemy arrows which had been dipped in pitch and lit on fire. The Word of God, often compared to water in Scripture, provides the chief ingredient in dousing arrows.

You may be tempted to ignore faith as something too vague or broad to grasp. Or you may consider faith simply an inventory of a person's religious beliefs. Yet faith is quite practical, providing an almost tangible piece of spiritual armor.

At the same time, faith means being "certain of what we do not see," according to Hebrews 11:1. We men are none too fond of those things we cannot see, hear, touch, taste, smell, measure, qualify, quantify, computerize, analyze, or synthesize. Suppose your wife spends two minutes talking to your female co-worker and later warns you to "watch out." You would probably be tempted to dismiss her hasty conclusion. Likewise, I have a hard time believing the claim of astrophysicists that more than ninety-nine percent of the universe is invisible. "Dark matter," they call it. You can't see the mass with a telescope, but it's out there.

Spiritual battles, too, are not physical or visible. They are spiritual and invisible, and our shield of faith functions on that same plane. So how does it deflect an arrow? How does it extinguish the flame? By the very nature of faith. Faith means believing that God's revelation of himself and your relationship with him is true, regardless of circumstantial evidence. Let's take another look at those earlier scenarios and see how you could defend yourself with the shield of faith.

- If you're tempted not to acknowledge your co-worker's role in a business project, believe that you are created in the image of God, who is complete truth. Your full identity is found in Christ; you don't need an extra jolt on the job at the expense of someone else. "Live as children of light (for the fruit of the light consists in all... truth)" (Ephesians 5:8-9).

- When you're tempted to curse a rude driver, believe that the new life of Christ in you has refashioned your mind, and therefore your speech. "Set a guard over my mouth, O Lord; keep watch over the door of my lips" (Psalm 141:3).

- When a consuming fear with some basis in reality wraps its tentacles around you, God wants to free you from anxiety. Grab the shield of faith and walk according to his command: "Do not be anxious about anything, but in everything, by prayer and petition, with thanksgiving, present your requests to God. And the peace of God, which transcends all understanding, will guard your hearts and your minds in Christ Jesus" (Philippians 4:6-7).

  Extinguish the arrows of fear with your faith, believing what Jesus taught in Matthew 6, that life amounts to more than meeting physical needs such as eating, drinking, and clothing. You don't need to worry because God will provide what you truly need. Jesus' concluding question gets right to the point of fighting the good fight of faith: "Who of you by worrying can add a single hour to his life?" (Matthew 6:27).

The shield of faith guards against not just arrows, but *flaming* arrows. An ordinary arrow can wound or kill as long as it strikes the right place. A flame-tipped arrow carries much more potential for destruction. It only needs to land on something flammable, and whoosh! James 3:5-10 helps us to understand this principal in reference to the dangerous potential of the tongue:

> Likewise the tongue is a small part of the body, but it makes great boasts. Consider what a great forest is set on fire by a

small spark. The tongue also is a fire, a world of evil among the parts of the body. It corrupts the whole person, sets the whole course of his life on fire, and is itself set on fire by hell. … With the tongue we praise our Lord and Father, and with it we curse men, who have been made in God's likeness. Out of the same mouth come praise and cursing. My brothers, this should not be.

Here we see Satan's scheme unveiled. If a flaming arrow of temptation lodges in the right spot, a match-sized flame can quickly grow to a disastrous conflagration. The obvious strategy on our part, then, is to extinguish the flame when it's small. If we remain vigilant, faith leaps in to douse the fire with the water of truth. Warning about the temptations of the adulteress, Proverbs 6:27 says, "Can a man scoop fire into his lap without his clothes being burned?" Don't let any flaming arrows linger. Don't toy with lust, greed, anger, bitterness, or any other temptation. Left alone, it will spread and consume you in flames.

KEEP THAT HELMET ON

I remember the joy of canoeing down a beautiful river in the Ozark Mountains of Arkansas. Occasional gray rock broke the monotony of the trees. Finally one cliff jutted out close enough to the river bank, beckoning so strongly that I stopped for a little rappelling. Within minutes I was slowly sliding down a rope, watching my feet and what was below. Suddenly a rock dislodged by the rope came crashing into the back of my head. With my one free hand, I touched the wound and beheld fingers full of blood and hair.

Had the rock struck anywhere else on my body, it would have brought blood and pain, but probably no life-threatening injury. Yet had it struck a different part of my skull, or hit with more force, I could have been dazed enough to release the rope, resulting in a dangerous fall. When I returned home from that trip, I remembered the mountain's message. I bought a climbing helmet. I never wanted to be caught off guard again by rough objects accelerating toward my head at thirty-two feet per second.

Neither did the apostle Paul want followers of Jesus to be caught off guard by Satan's deadly missiles. Like a highway patrolman preaching the use of safety belts to an apathetic public, he encouraged his readers to be active, to make full use of the available safety equipment: *"Take* the helmet of salvation" (Ephesians 6:17). And by all means, keep it on.

Why did Paul link salvation with defense of the head? Salvation marks our transferral from the kingdom of darkness to the kingdom of light, a change no less dramatic than that between day and night. Yet our perception of how much salvation means to us can diminish, especially over time. Satan uses every means at his disposal to aid that process. We must wear the helmet of salvation to deflect the doubt and cynicism he shoots our way. For example:

- You begin to notice your church's primary adult Sunday school teacher subtly displaying pride in ways that contradict what he teaches.

- You hear a friend talking about how he and his wife prayed for their ill child, but she died.

- You try to remember when you last sensed the reality of God during prayer or worship. The recollections are so fuzzy and blended together that you wonder if your relationship with God is genuine.

The elemental truths of salvation form the foundation of your Christian walk, the cornerstone of your fortress against the arrows of doubt. Having come under the lordship of Christ, you need not be sidetracked by expecting perfection from any Sunday school teacher, pastor, or televangelist. All have sinned—and continue to sin—falling short of the glory of God. Those who share that same salvation are co-laborers with you in Christ. Resist any fiery dart that tempts you to criticize your brothers and sisters. Instead, love them. Pray for them. Look for opportunities to admonish, encourage, and show compassion to all in need.

Your salvation is based on what Christ has done for you by dying on the cross, not on what he may do for you in the future. Resist the temptation to doubt him simply because you've been disappointed. Even though Jesus healed many sick people when he walked the earth, he acted selectively. He would not be tested by anyone then, and he will not be put to the test now.

Salvation never depends on our feelings, past or present, even though you may have been deeply touched at the time you received Christ. Perhaps you had bottomed out after a long courtship with alcohol, or you may have been flailing about in a deep pool of depression. Maybe tears came to your eyes as you surrendered willful control of your life. You may have sensed the infilling of something new, the way a drink of cold water feels going down a parched throat.

Then again, maybe you didn't feel anything. God calls people in different ways, but their salvation is the same. We all serve the same God, who has not changed and will not change. On many occasions God does not—or so it seems to us—answer prayers, respond to our worship, or draw alongside of us during trouble. Just as a wise parent gradually weans a child from constant dependency, God wants to mature us so that we can fight with confidence—knowing our place in his army, heeding his orders, feeling secure in our salvation. The helmet of salvation can screen our eyes, ears, and brain from the arrows that would damage our confidence in Christ.

NO ORDINARY SWORD

The first five pieces of armor are primarily defensive or utilitarian: belt, breastplate, shoes, shield, and helmet. The sword, too, can be defensive, deflecting blows in hand-to-hand combat. But the sword stands out as being distinctly offensive. It penetrates. It slices open. It wounds. It kills. As a spiritual weapon, God "uses it to cut through people's defenses, to prick their consciences and to stab them spiritually awake. Yet he also puts his sword into our hands, so that we may use it both in resisting temptation... and in evangelism."[3]

Paul used the image of a sword to illustrate the Word of God. The Greek word here is *rhema*, meaning Scripture brought to mind for a specific instance, or God speaking to someone in a fresh way for a given circumstance. The Greek word *logos* is generally used in the New Testament when referring to God's word as revealed through Scripture. The first Jewish believers had the books of the Old Testament, which prophesied the coming of Messiah. Modern-day believers also have access to the New Testament, where Jesus is described as the Word of God made flesh.

These two Greek words are not unrelated. Unless your mind and spirit are regularly feeding on Scripture (*logos*), the Holy Spirit will find little to stimulate. And much of the *rhema* which God imparts—through teaching or writing, or in a direct word or encouragement or rebuke from a friend—is based on Scripture, utilizes Scripture, and certainly must agree with scriptural principles.

Because of this close connection, a passage regarding the *logos*-word may help us to understand the potential of the *rhema*-word as a weapon: "For the word of God is living and active. Sharper than any double-edged sword, it penetrates even to dividing soul and spirit, joints and marrow; it judges the thoughts and attitudes of the heart" (Hebrews 4:12).

Living and active. How powerful God's word is! Using this sword involves far more than just quoting God's rules to the enemy, or using the "right" words in prayer. Make no mistake: God wants us to grasp this spiritual sword and do something with it. At the same time, the sword is no inert weapon depending on our fencing skills to be effective. God supercharged this sword before he placed it in our scabbard. Think of biological warfare: releasing live germs able to cause destruction on their own. Or a heat-seeking missile: a weapon that operates independently once it's fired. "All Scripture is God-breathed and is useful for teaching, rebuking, correcting, and training in righteousness, so that the man of God may be thoroughly equipped for every good work" (2 Timothy 3:16).

Judges the thoughts and attitudes. Hebrews 4 also says that God's Word is "sharper than any double-edged sword," so sharp that it penetrates to the depths of our being. In a way that nothing else can, God's Word discerns our attitude and judges whether or not it is godly.

The Book of Acts describes an episode where the sword was wielded in the early church. The gospel was spreading so rapidly that many believers sold all their belongings to help support the entire church. Ananias and Sapphira sold a piece of property and gave most of the proceeds to the church, but decided to hold back part of it for themselves. When they brought the money to Peter, Ananias lied by claiming they were contributing the entire amount. The issue wasn't the money—which they were free to do with as they chose—but one of deception. Perhaps Ananias and his wife wanted to impress everyone with their generosity.

God filled Peter with a *rhema*-word for the moment: "Ananias, how is it that Satan has so filled your heart that you have lied to the Holy Spirit and have kept for yourself some of the money you received for the land? Didn't it belong to you before it was sold? And after it was sold, wasn't the money at your disposal? What made you think of doing such a thing? You have not lied to men but to God." When Ananias heard this rebuke, he fell down and died (Acts 5:3-5).

When his wife showed up three hours later, she repeated the same lie. Peter confronted her with the same charge. Sapphira, too, dropped dead. God's Word was powerfully active through Peter, literally dividing soul from spirit. How many times do we ourselves struggle against deception, wanting to pretend that we're doing something that we're not? We especially want to maintain the appearance of spirituality by doing good deeds which others can see.

The truth often proves unpleasant. Sometimes we have to remind ourselves that God knows the full extent of our selfishness. His eye detects the unholy mixture of motives that can defile our sincerest attempts to please him. All God asks is that we be honest with him, honest with ourselves, and make the best of the spiritual equipment he has made available, including the sword of the Spirit. Just remember: Its blade isolates both what is good and what is unholy.

Simply possessing spiritual armor and weapons no more makes you an effective warrior than having a complete football uniform makes you a star quarterback. You need training. Be assured that God will give you plenty of opportunities for practice and growth in your call to fight for the kingdom of righteousness.

FIVE

Developing Battlefield Reflexes

S TUCK IN THE OUTFIELD during a men's softball game, I began to marvel over how God has wired our bodies. How is it that in a fraction of a second after the batter raps a long fly ball, my legs are moving? How do those legs know whether to move right or left? When the ball has barely begun its ascent, how do they know whether to go forward or backward?

The simple answer is that the brain immediately interprets the visual perceptions and sends instructions by way of the nervous system to the appropriate leg muscles. Yet this tremendously complex interaction can take place almost without any discernible deliberation. A ballplayer who wasted much time and energy consciously analyzing each play would probably fail. Seasoned ballplayers who have made the same kind of play so many times before almost seem to cruise in on automatic pilot to put away a routine pop fly.

Such lightning-quick mental calculations combined with habitual muscular responses are what we call reflexes. While we typically use this word to describe involuntary movements such as a knee jerk, *Webster's Seventh New Collegiate Dictionary* also defines reflex as "the power of acting or responding with adequate speed, or an habitual and predictable way of thinking and behaving." Professional athletes earn millions by developing reflexes to levels of perfection.

Musicians achieve success according to the same principle. Classical pianists who perform at Carnegie Hall are not consciously thinking of every note in every chord in every bar of music. They *learned* the score note by note, chord by chord, line by line, and then dedicated themselves to endless practice. Gradually the mass of notes were transformed into a team effort of eyes, ears, and hands moving reflexively—quickly, habitually, predictably—through an extremely complex linear progression.

The military also utilizes trained habits by trying to instill certain responses into new recruits. We've all heard horror stories of basic training: awful tales of pre-dawn awakenings by a barking drill sergeant, interminable jogs while sweltering under full combat gear, grueling exercise periods, and timed sprints through muddy, cumbersome obstacle courses. Through all of this training, the army hopes to produce a man whose body can sustain pain and perform at a certain level of combat, a man who obeys orders promptly and thoroughly, a man who can be a good team player on and off the battlefield.

God's expectations aren't much different. He wants men who can discipline their bodies, refraining from what's ungodly and pursuing what's godly. He wants men who are eager to learn his will, as expressed in the Bible, and carry it out. Whether they happen to be new Christians, isolated Christians, or mature Christians with a recognized ministry, God wants men humble enough to realize their need for being part of a church and accountable to other men.

GOD'S BASIC TRAINING

A reflexive behavior shows up in your immediate response to a stimulus, lots of which cross your path in any given day. How you habitually respond depends largely on your spiritual training. Those reflexes are formed in many ways as you are "discipled," or trained, throughout your Christian walk. Much of that training will depend on other people and external sources—such as church doctrine, church teaching, home meetings, Christian reading, and broadcast ministries.

The rest of the reflex development depends on you—what might be called ongoing basic training. Two difficulties, though. One is that no ornery sergeant stays on your case to keep you moving forward. The other is that gauging your progress can be difficult, even to the point of discouragement. Spiritual training comes with no objective measuring rod. And one of the key goals is none too palatable to us competitive males: to advance others at our expense. The apostle Paul wrote, "In humility consider others better than yourselves" (Philippians 2:3).

If you insist on being a career Christian, Satan's preferences aren't hard to identify. He hopes you'll be—in a spiritual sense —office-bound and pot-bellied, thinking that you've got this religious thing licked, and assuming that spiritual training is for rookies.

Let's examine four areas of ongoing basic training that will help you avoid that slouching posture to which our fleshly nature naturally inclines: a daily meeting with God, fasting, fellowship, and accountability. By employing these crucial disciplines, you can continually strengthen your defensive and offensive reflexes. With this training and outfitted with the spiritual armor described in the last chapter, you will be better prepared to fight when Satan fires his flaming arrows.

GETTING TO KNOW YOU

When my wife and I were dating, we often had rambling late night talks that turned into early morning talks. Walking along the Mississippi River or chowing down in an all-night deli, we reveled in getting to know one another. Other married couples can tell similar stories. Yet long after the infatuation of early romance has faded—as any counselor will tell you—couples must keep up regular, meaningful communication to maintain a growing, healthy marital relationship.

You also have a relationship with God. Do you communicate with him only on Sunday morning? Only when you flub up and need a quick fix? Only when you say grace before a meal or pray with your children at bedtime? If you have a wife or steady girlfriend, would she be satisfied if you granted her no more communication time than you have given God?

Some men decide to keep at least a minimum of regularity in their relationship with God by reading the Bible daily. Some choose to "feed" on God's Word every day before feeding on breakfast. While this sort of discipline can bear good fruit, it carries some pitfalls. First, it offers no guarantee that you will grow closer to God, just as success with any outward discipline offers no proof of spiritual maturity. Second, such a routine is not for everyone, nor is it the only way to cultivate the kind of spiritual reflexes God wants in his warriors. And third, it can lull you into a works-oriented approach to pleasing God, including unnecessary guilt when you fail to keep your commitment. In other words, Satan can twist your success with self-discipline into false success, as well as blow up your lack of self-discipline into condemnation.

So much for the warning. Here's the good side. A daily, private time with the Lord is somewhat like a church service in combining three complementary components: Bible reading (with some study and meditation or memorization), worship, and prayer. As you spend time with the Lord, his likeness, his concerns, his thoughts, and his character are increasingly imparted to you. When questioned about his ministry and that of the emerging Messiah, John the Baptist said: "I must decrease; he must increase." That should be your goal, as well.

Even if you could recite every book of the Bible and teach eloquently about them, you would not be assured of striking the first blow in spiritual warfare. But the *life* of Jesus, as it grows in you, can move mountains. The challenge in a daily time of communion with God is to feed that new, inner man. Help it to grow while the old, outer man shrinks. God's desire is not that you learn how to *act* more religious, but that the new life within you grows more powerful. Paul put it this way: "I pray that out of his glorious riches he may strengthen you with power through his Spirit in your inner being, so that Christ may dwell in your hearts through faith" (Ephesians 3:16-17).

FAITHFUL IN SOWING

I don't mean to imply that this daily transformation process is supposed to come as easily as chewing the fat with a good friend over coffee. Spiritual training does not come naturally. Just as in the real army, basic training can be a very rude awakening to the cocky recruit who only last week had the world in his back pocket. You're looking for habits or disciplines in the natural realm that will produce benefits in the supernatural realm—your spirit communing with God, who is a spirit.

Jesus said, "God is spirit, and his worshipers must worship in spirit and in truth" (John 4:24). If you've ever tried a daily devotional time, you know there are days when you feel like you've been reading the phone book and talking to yourself. Yet even those times can be valuable. From God's perspective, they show our desire to draw close to him, as best we know how, no matter how distant he may seem. Such faithfulness demonstrates our unconditional love for God, without being dependent upon a particular response.

And who knows whether your Bible reading or study will bear unexpected fruit? Financial planners stress regularity in savings to achieve the best results; accumulating knowledge of Scripture on a regular basis usually produces the best results. Ecclesiastes 11:6 advises, "Sow your seed in the morning, and at evening let not your hands be idle, for you do not know which will succeed, whether this or that, or whether both will do equally well." God's Word is compared in the Bible to seed.

Whether it is sown in the brilliant sunshine of a gifted teacher, or in the darkness of a drab personal quiet time, the seed of his Word will still sprout in your spirit to show forth his glory.

I offer no recommendation as to how long you should spend in daily personal time with God. Biographies of the spiritual giants of Christianity reveal many who spent hours every day praying and reading the Bible. Don't consider that a standard for yourself. I only advise that you try to make it a part of your daily schedule, such as early morning or before bedtime.

If you've never tried such a routine, keep it short, at least for a while. Even a few minutes can be fruitful. Ideally, you will sense a little spark of divine romance which makes you crave more time with your first love, reading about God and communing with him in ways that become ever more natural.

Don't be put off by all the cares and distractions of life. Worries about your job, difficult decisions that are looming, problems with a friend or family member—you can bring all of these before your heavenly Father, who cares about the smallest of details. How much better to have an appointed time to meet with the ultimate Counselor than to just careen through life, vainly hoping that your Christianity, like an exclusive credit card, carries privileges that will get you through any uncertainty.

READY TO RESPOND

On a surface level, I hope you will make a daily meeting with God a sort of lifestyle habit, like brushing your teeth at certain times. But you can expect more important changes in your behavior and attitudes to happen as a result of that investment.

Trouble with a foul mouth? As you start putting more and more Scripture through your mind and into your spirit, it begins to fill your heart. Jesus said that the mouth speaks out of that which fills the heart. As the inner man increases and the fleshly nature decreases, you gradually succeed in replacing an old pattern of cursing with one of renewed speech.

Let's suppose you've been praying regularly about sharing your faith with a certain co-worker. When the Holy Spirit unexpectedly opens a conversational door just a crack, you'll be more attuned to the opportunity and enter in with confidence. When spiritually prepared, you may respond almost without thinking. On the other hand, if you've been neglecting your ongoing basic training, you may be too preoccupied with marital difficulties or just too disgruntled with this particular guy to even recognize the opening of a garage door big enough for a Mack truck to drive through.

Dave had a Christian friend who was extremely anxious over the trials and distresses of a pending divorce, especially child custody and property distribution. His friend needed an open invitation to draw upon God's wisdom. Dave pointed him toward James 1:2-5: "Consider it pure joy, my brothers, whenever you face trials of many kinds, because you know that the testing of your faith develops perseverance. Perseverance must finish its work so that you may be mature and complete, not lacking anything. If any of you lacks wisdom, he should ask God, who gives generously to all without finding fault, and it will be given to him."

Dave said, "It was an incredible revelation that God could use this to make him perfect and complete, lacking in nothing." His friend also began to see the cumulative fruits of his own bad decisions. "He said, 'I can't believe that I went through fifty years of life and that all my wisdom was for nothing.' Those three verses have changed his life as far as knowing God."

You may not think of yourself as a counselor or a minister, but you are. God didn't save you to turn you into a holy trophy gathering dust in a display case. He wants to turn you into a fountain of life, overflowing into the lives of others beset by the same spiritual warfare.

Where do you begin to develop these battlefield reflexes? You have to begin somewhere. Your pastor can't make you do it. Your best friend can't make you do it. Your wife can't make you do it. (Although they all might try.) But if you take the first steps, however small, God is eager to become your partner in the business of changing you into his likeness.

FASTING

Fasting is prayer with an attitude. One attitude in particular: humility. There is nothing spiritual about empty stomachs. God's arm can't be twisted by hunger strikes. Fasting needs to be coupled with prayer in order to be effective.

Around 460 B.C., when the exiled Jews were under the rule of Persia, the king issued an edict for their annihilation to be carried out on a certain day. The Jews mourned and fasted when they heard the news. One of their own, Esther, had become queen under unusual circumstances. Esther decided that she and her maids would fast three days and sent word to the Jews to do the same. While prayer isn't specifically mentioned in the book of Esther, it was most likely included during this crisis, just as the Hebrews prayed during other periods of fasting.

Talk about spiritual warfare! This was a major assault, an all-out offensive on the part of Satan. A civil decree was days away from wiping out God's chosen race. The strategy of a corporate fast paid off. Haman, the king's right-hand man who had originally devised the genocide plan, was exposed as an egotistical anti-Semite. The king reversed the decree and had Haman hanged on the very gallows intended for Esther's uncle, Mordecai.

Fine, you may think, I'll be ready to fast next time a Hitler-like despot threatens to kill all Christians. Actually, fasting is quite appropriate in less sensational situations.

For example, the Hebrews didn't reserve fasting for crises. The Day of Atonement was an annual fast day stipulated in Leviticus 16:29 and 31. Tradition later added other fast days to the calendar. Jesus said during the Sermon on the Mount, *"When* you fast… ,"* not *"If* you fast." A fast certainly doesn't have to be for three days or even a full day. If you regularly eat three meals a day, skipping even one meal can constitute a fast.

It's advisable to take in plenty of fluids for health reasons, though you don't want to fall into the trap of gorging yourself with enough fruit juice or soft drinks or milk to stave off hunger pains. That gnawing in your stomach should serve a more important purpose than simply reminding you of the scrambled eggs you missed at breakfast time, or the potato chips your co-worker is munching. (Why is it you never noticed you could *smell* potato chips?)

Physical hunger reminds you of why you're doing what you're doing. You are humbling your body—making it lower, subordinating it to your spirit and your spiritual aims. Although he was speaking in terms broader than fasting, the apostle Paul said, "I beat my body and make it my slave" (1 Corinthians 9:27). Anything you can do to subjugate the cravings of your flesh can help to put your spirit more in control—right where it needs to be for effective spiritual warfare.

However long a fast is, be sure to plan some time alone to concentrate on prayer. A longer period of prayer is ideal, though that's not always possible. At least try to replace regular food with feeding on God's Word and presence at your usual meal time.

Why should you add fasting to your prayer? What sort of results can you expect? Fasting is mentioned several times in the New Testament, but with little elaboration. In the classic passage on fasting, Isaiah sets forth the proper attitude and purpose of fasting, in contrast to the hypocritical and showy fasts of his day. The prophet also presents the glorious breakthrough that can occur as a result of fasting with a right heart.

> Is not this the kind of fasting I have chosen: to loose the chains of injustice and untie the cords of the yoke, to set the oppressed free and break every yoke?... the glory of the Lord will be your rear guard. Then you will call, and the Lord will answer; you will cry for help and he will say: Here am I....

Your people will rebuild the ancient ruins and will raise up the age-old foundations; you will be called Repairer of Broken Walls, Restorer of Streets with Dwellings.   Isaiah 58:6-12

Notice the words which hint of warfare and post-warfare: chains, cords of bondage, yokes of oppression. Such language speaks of the handiwork of Satan. He wants you not merely to go wading into the shallow waters of sin, only to jump right out and repent, but to become totally immersed in a deep hole of sin. Satan wants to lead you around like a dumb ox, having to trudge through each day yoked to the same old sin that you cannot shake, no matter how hard you try.

WEEDING OUT HYPOCRISY

You may launch into a fast for a specific purpose, pleading with God to act in power, as Esther did. Or you may be seeking guidance about some particular decision. Either way, because of having humbled yourself, be prepared for God to speak to you in a surprising way.

Two men in full-time ministry agreed to a prolonged fast and committed much of their time to reading the Book of Psalms. "A really weird thing happened in our praying," Bruce said. Both men noticed that the psalms which asked God to smite the wicked began to take on a new meaning. The usual sense of cheering God on to clobber the enemies of Christianity, always the other guys, no longer applied. "God turned it around and said, 'Your will, your arrogance, your pride need to be dealt with,'" Bruce said.

Have you ever noticed God's tendency to hold the mirror in front of you when you point an accusing finger at others? Entering into a fast with you as the "good guy" and someone else as the "bad guy" treads on very swampy ground. Isaiah casts a different light on proper fasting by placing an equal stress on righteous behavior:

Is it not to share your food with the hungry and to provide the poor wanderer with shelter—when you see the naked, to clothe him, and not to turn away from your own flesh and blood?... If you do away with the yoke of oppression, with the pointing finger and malicious talk, and if you spend yourselves in behalf of the hungry and satisfy the needs of the oppressed, then....   Isaiah 58:7-10

Then good things will come, but that's a mighty big "if" on the front end. Because God is holy, he wants his people to aspire to a life free of hypocrisy, a relationship with him that cannot be reduced to a simple formula of keeping the stomach empty, all the while leaving the heart full of sin.

This "if... then" connection is followed by enough bait to enable even the weakest, hungriest faster to complete his spiritual journey. In addition to loosing the bondage of injustice and oppression—whether personal or churchwide—Isaiah specifies several other motivations and expectations regarding fasting:

- *Spiritual healing and God's protection:* "Then your light will break forth like the dawn, and your healing will quickly appear; then your righteousness will go before you, and the glory of the Lord will be your rear guard" (58:8).

- *Answered prayer and God's vivid presence:* "Then you will call, and the Lord will answer; you will cry for help, and he will say: Here am I" (58:9).

- *Godly guidance:* "The Lord will guide you always" (58:11).

- *Strength and prosperity:* God "will satisfy your needs in a sun-scorched land and will strengthen your frame. You will be like a well-watered garden, like a spring whose waters never fail" (58:11).

- *Restoration of community and culture:* "Your people will rebuild the ancient ruins and will raise up the age-old foundations; you will be called Repairer of Broken Walls, Restorer of Streets with Dwellings" (58:12).

Along with a daily quiet time with the Lord, fasting can be an invaluable element of spiritual warfare. Your basic training as a warrior for Christ won't be complete without it. You never know when your spiritual reflexes will be called upon. Whenever you especially need God's protection, guidance in a major decision, or radical renewal in your life, family, church, city, or nation—prayer mixed with fasting can unleash God's power.

Furthermore, fasting will enhance the positive personal habits developed through daily communion with God. Denying yourself food for the sake of the kingdom of God helps to shrink the fleshly part of you that craves comfort, familiarity, and pleasure. As you couple fasting with prayer, you become more and more dominated by the spiritual side, which craves fellowship with Christ, conformity to his nature, and the increase of his kingdom in our midst.

As powerful as prayer and fasting are, the ongoing basic training of the normal Christian life needs more than these inner disciplines. The second two elements can be met only through banding together with other believers.

FELLOWSHIP

An earlier chapter touched on 1 Peter 5:8: "Your enemy the devil prowls around like a roaring lion looking for someone to devour." Anyone who's ever seen a nature documentary about lions on the plains of Africa knows that they don't go after the fleetest gazelles who are able to run with the pack. Instead, these wily hunters pick out the weak, the injured, the old, the young.

Just like a lion, Satan watches while he prowls. If he notices that you're a lone ranger who avoids companionship with Christian friends and casually skips church services, the devil puts you at the top of his menu.

War is not a superstar event. Battles are won by large armies, where everyone knows his own job and how to support and rescue those at his side. Weakness in Christian fellowship can put any man in spiritual danger, but single men who live alone are often even more vulnerable. One responded to a message I posted on a computer bulletin board soliciting thoughts on spiritual warfare. This single man leads a small fellowship, yet still feels short on allies in the war.

"There are not very many twenty-four-year-olds who are sold out to God and would like to get together and pray," he wrote. "There is always church, but no one to pray with on a daily basis for stability." Whether married or single, you need fellowship for several reasons:

The Bible commands us to spend time with other believers. "Let us not give up meeting together, as some are in the habit of doing, but let us encourage one another" (Hebrews 10:25). Don't interpret this as narrowly referring to a Sunday service. Whenever you and another brother in Christ get together—and it should be more frequently than weekly—you've got a meeting.

Fellowship will help keep you out of trouble. Proverbs 13:20 says, "He who walks with the wise grows wise, but a companion of fools suffers harm." A typically vain man likes to think that he directs his own path, uninfluenced by others. The truth is, we are all affected by those with whom we fellowship.

Certain situations, especially on the job, provide abundant opportunities to associate with unbelievers. You can either take advantage of those times by reaching out to others, or you can let them drag you down into the muck of worldliness. At other times you may deliberately seek out men who are lost, hoping to find an open door for the gospel or to build a relationship that could lead to opportunities to witness. But don't kid yourself into thinking that you need no Christian fellowship at all. You need your brothers in Christ, and your times together can help all of you stay on the straight and narrow.

Fellowship builds up God's army. "And let us consider how we may spur one another on toward love and good deeds"

(Hebrews 10:24). When people don't see each other very often, it's hard for them to stimulate one another to do deeds of love and kindness, whether for one another or for those outside the church.

Regular fellowship encourages us to stand against Satan. We all have weaknesses. But we can minimize our solo struggles by spending time with other Christians, both in formal meetings and in simply passing time with friends. Satan knows your weaknesses and will exploit them as much as you allow him to. The church gathers people who know they have a fallen nature and allows them to circle the wagons against that voracious lion who is always prowling to catch them alone and off guard. James 4:7 promises that if we resist the devil, he will flee from us. Our resistance becomes much more effective when we are joined to others.

Fellowship promotes Christian maturity. Even if you spend time alone reading the Bible and other Christian books, your growth in spiritual maturity is sharply limited. For one thing, the more you dabble in dogma by yourself, the greater the potential for error. Warning about false teaching and deceitful men, the apostle Paul offered this alternative: "Instead, speaking the truth in love, we will in all things grow up into him who is the Head, that is, Christ. From whom the whole body, joined and held together by every supporting ligament, grows and builds itself up in love, as each part does its work" (Ephesians 4:15-16).

The normal Christian life includes functioning as a part of the body of Christ. We will never go far in basic Christian training without that crucial link to the central processing unit, the head, who is Christ. No part of the body is of much use all by itself; but together, every part can mature as it "grows and builds itself up in love, as each part does its work."

ACCOUNTABILITY

Another valuable aspect of fellowship falls more precisely under the fourth area of training: accountability. Paul admonishes, "Do not think of yourself more highly than you ought, but rather think of yourself with sober judgment, in accordance with the measure of faith God has given you" (Romans 12:3). Do you get the impression that man's ego will inflate quicker than an automobile air bag? You know it will.

Our tendency toward pride and self-sufficiency is reflected in thinking we've got everything under control. Sure, we blow it here and there, but we're no fools. We can see that. We're busy plugging the holes, getting our act together, keeping it on the road, and all of that. Satan, meanwhile, is busily scheming how to keep us thinking this way. He will try anything to dilute our self-judgment, away from being "sober." Deception is Satan's game, and if our fleshly nature also inclines toward deception, so much the better.

The Bible warns of our need for accountability in less than gentle terms. "Wounds from a friend can be trusted, but an enemy multiplies kisses" (Proverbs 27:6). "As iron sharpens iron, so one man sharpens another" (Proverbs 27:17). Getting wounded or being ground against an iron file doesn't sound very pleasant, does it? Sometimes it's not. Yet iron filings occasionally fall from the "filing cabinets" of accountability. Many Christian men will tell you they could not have continued on their path toward maturity without the regular, private, candid input of another man or a small group of men. I have personally benefited from this sort of help, especially in my early Christian walk.

How does accountability work? On a simple, informal level, it involves finding a friend whose maturity and judgment you trust enough to solicit frank feedback on your life. You welcome this person's comments on your tough decisions, as well as on your progress as a Christian warrior fighting the good fight of faith on every front.

On a more formal level, you could receive accountability through a weekly or monthly meeting with a small group of trusted men with similar beliefs. Though levels of intimacy and detail may need to be curbed when more than two people are gathered, you can still hold one another accountable to standards of openness and self-discipline.

Some of these groups confess sins to one another, in accordance with James 5:16: "Therefore confess your sins to each other and pray for each other so that you may be healed." Two positive effects are thereby set into motion. First, of course, is the healing process, which ultimately comes from God. Second, knowing that in good conscience you will need to openly admit sins to others provides marvelous incentive to refrain from sin.

Other than the matter of seeking counsel for important decisions, how can you benefit from accountability?

Your relationship with God: If you're like most men, you're much readier to discuss externals—how well-integrated you are in church programs, how regular you've been with Bible reading, or how many verses you've memorized. While those kinds of issues have their place, you can become too comfortable using them to cover up real problems. You need to be open about whether a true relationship with God even exists. Is it open and flowing both ways? Can you point to an area where God is molding you? Is the relationship regular, or is it limited to an emergency-only basis?

Your work: Are you serving your employer (and employees, if that applies) as unto the Lord? Are your decisions in conformity with biblical ethics?

Your money: Are you being a wise steward? Staying out of debt or at least moving in that direction? Tithing?

Lust: Don't get bogged down in discussing temptation. Zero in on where you're failing to take those thoughts captive to Christ (2 Corinthians 10:5) or where you're allowing yourself to be placed in compromising situations that look bad or could lead to serious trouble.

Because of their life-long commitment, married men need accountability in two additional areas in order to stay battle-ready rather than battle-weary:

Your relationship with your wife: Are you giving her the time, attention, affection, and love she needs? Are you carving out time alone with her? Are you nurturing her emotionally and spiritually according to Ephesians 5?

Your relationship with your children: Are you giving them the time, attention, affection, and love they need? Are you training them in the ways of the Lord, according to Deuteronomy 6? Are you presenting an image of God the Father that will attract them? Are you providing as much of the discipline as possible in order to make your wife's life more tolerable?

Implementing these suggestions in no way means that you turn your life over to another man or to a group. You succeed and fail as an individual. God covets his relationship with every one of his children. After all the counsel and prayer has been put into your internal blender, never let human wisdom take precedence over the deepest conviction of your heart. Doing so would amount to idolatry. God would rather have you obey your own conscience—as long as it wouldn't violate Scripture —than to obey the voice of a human being out of spiritual laziness or fear of others.

Accountability needs to become a trained habit of the serious Christian warrior. Suppose you were hiking along a mountain path and began to drift off the trail. Your trained eye would soon steer your legs back to where the path was smooth and clear trail markers pointed the way. Accountability serves that same function on our spiritual journey. Even though we men are famous for trying to get anywhere without asking for directions or help, it's nice now and then to have a trusted friend tell us exactly how right—or wrong—we are.

Having looked at basic training and the reflexes we want to develop, along with the armor and weapons God has granted, let's turn to the major battlefield of our thought life.

SIX

The War Raging in Your Mind

W ITH A LOT ON HIS MIND ALREADY, Michael got a phone call at work that only made matters worse. A colonel would be visiting the Army Reserve unit for which Michael was responsible, and he was expecting a briefing. The worries began to ricochet inside his skull: "Why is he coming down? What's he upset about?" As the unbridled speculation continued, Michael finally realized that he was losing any sense of peace as well as the ability to focus on his job.

"Wait a minute," he told himself. "I'm all worked up over nothing."

Battling his fear of the unknown took about an hour. Michael's best weapon for this skirmish was a word spoken by God through the apostle Paul: "we are destroying speculations and... taking every thought captive to the obedience of Christ" (2 Corinthians 10:5, NAS). Michael incorporated this verse into his prayer: "Father, I ask your forgiveness for allowing speculation to enter in. By your word you've spoken, I am going to destroy speculations by taking every thought captive to the obedience of Christ. Thank you for helping me to lay this down and go about my business."

In a practical sense, Michael regained his perspective. He

was able to turn this potential worry over the colonel's visit into something positive. "I tried to look at it as a plus—thank goodness he's coming, and he'll share his concerns face to face," he said. "And I have some concerns he hasn't really heard."

Spiritual battles can take place on various levels, as succeeding chapters will show. Let's examine one of the most basic: the mind. Thoughts bring pleasure, pain, memories, and innumerable emotions. Our minds can envision at least some inkling of what God is like. They are equally capable of erecting a wall between God and us.

How well Satan knows this. Some would argue, with good reason, that the mind is his favorite battleground. Or to quote a popular saying, an idle mind is the devil's playground. Satan is a master propagandist, knowing just which thoughts to plant and when to plant them. He is diligent to oil those mental cogs that would have us doubt God's existence, God's promises, what God has done for his people throughout history, and what God has done in our own lives.

Fortunately, God did not make us like factory robots, blindly performing the same task over and over, controlled by someone's programming. Instead, he gave us the ability to seize thoughts and evaluate them. This ability is a key part of spiritual warfare, as Paul explains: "For though we live in the world, we do not wage war as the world does. The weapons we fight with are not the weapons of the world. On the contrary, they have divine power to demolish strongholds. We demolish arguments and every pretension that sets itself up against the knowledge of God, and we take captive every thought to make it obedient to Christ" (2 Corinthians 10:3-5).

Most of our spiritual struggles begin with the thought life. And as the vocabulary of this passage shows—"wage war," "weapons," "demolish," "strongholds," "take captive"—we are engaged in real warfare, with real winners and losers. Being victorious means scrutinizing our thoughts and making sure they conform to godliness. Sadly, when we fail to seize ungodly thoughts, we cede loss in too many areas for too long. The defeat becomes painfully evident in failed marriages, ruined careers, or tarnished personal integrity.

MENTAL FOOTHOLDS

Serious rock climbers wear footwear somewhat like high-topped athletic shoes, except with the unusual feature of a fairly rigid sole. That firmness allows the climber to support his entire body on the slimmest foothold, a bit of rock that extends perhaps no more than a quarter inch from an otherwise smooth face. I'm no serious climber, but I have climbed enough to appreciate a good foothold. With it, the climber moves on to greater and greater heights; without it, an attempted ascent can be totally stopped, even at a low level.

The apostle Paul appreciated footholds, too, though in a spiritual sense. "Do not give the devil a foothold," he warned in Ephesians 4:27. The problem with a foothold, of course, is that it leads to a stronghold. Our thought life is the perfect place for Satan to establish a foothold for several reasons:

Thoughts seem harmless. Your resentment of an ambitious co-worker may be sinful, but easy to rationalize. After all, your peers criticize other company personnel. How can a certain amount of friction be avoided?

Thoughts are hidden. Sexual fantasies, lofty flights of pride, baseless fears—how embarrassing if others could rent a video-tape of your secret mind games!

Thoughts do not introduce themselves by saying where they originated. Immediate sensory input—what you're hearing, seeing, and doing at the moment—probably constitutes the bulk of a day's thought life. When driving alone, for example, memory, music, or a deliberate train of thought, such as planning a weekend trip, may dictate thought life. Yet whether or not you're mentally occupied, whether or not you've been making a strong effort to draw close to God, you remain vulnerable to Satan's fiery darts. He is constantly looking for ways to slip the right thought into your consciousness. Knowing that you may not discern where a particular thought came from, Satan seeks to gain a foothold in your mind.

Thoughts are too numerous to count. From the time we first crawl out of bed to the moment we collapse in the same place many hours later, most men stay pretty busy. Dealing with a job, socializing, perhaps handling the myriad duties that come with a family—all these activities are more than enough to keep one's head buzzing. Even if you wanted to scrutinize every thought as to its place of origin—God, Satan, or some neutral ground—doing so would be very difficult.

Difficult, but not impossible. Otherwise God would not have commanded that "we take captive *every* thought to make it obedient to Christ" (2 Corinthians 10:5). How can you practically carry out this command? One way would be to turn inward, obsessively focusing on every thought that crosses your mind. This would be like taking a fly swatter to an open garbage dumpster in mid-summer. The more realistic goal is to keep yourself on the path toward Christlikeness, constantly being conformed to his character, having a mind that is being continually renewed.

You can also understand God's command to "take captive every thought to make it obedient to Christ" in terms of lordship. Because Christ is Lord, the innermost part of your being is to be subject to him. The more developed that relationship, the more attuned you are to what thoughts float through your mind. Whenever Satan tries to slip one of his booby-trapped little rafts into your stream of consciousness, your inner alarm should sound a warning.

A BUDDING STRONGHOLD

On a simple level, your conscience works as an inner alarm system. Maybe you feel tempted to gossip about someone. You know the information doesn't need to be shared, so your conscience flashes a red light. Then it's your choice. You still have to exercise the power of your will one way or another.

But this matter of establishing footholds and strongholds is often more subtle, with consequences that are virtually unlimited. Consider the example of King David in 2 Samuel 11:

> In the spring, at the time when kings go off to war, David sent Joab out with the king's men and the whole Israelite army.... One evening David got up from his bed and walked around on the roof of the palace. From the roof he saw a woman bathing. The woman was very beautiful, and David sent someone to find out about her. The man said, "Isn't this Bathsheba...?" Then David sent messengers to get her. She came to him, and he slept with her.... The woman conceived.... 2 Samuel 11:1-5

Though he had risen to power as a great military leader, David chose not to go off to war in the spring, as kings usually did. Instead, we find him hanging around the palace and ogling Bathsheba, like a man with too much time on his hands and too little responsibility. If, indeed, King David should have been on the battlefield, his decision to stay home was the first step in giving the devil a foothold in his life.

When David saw Bathsheba, he wasn't wrong to think of her as attractive. Being tempted to lust is common to every man. Perhaps he was still struggling with temptation, feeling stuck in a state of ambivalence, when he sent someone to find out the woman's identity. Yet that action increased Satan's foothold in David's heart. Even after David left his rooftop, he knew his messenger would remind him of the woman. It turned out that she was a married woman whose husband had gone to war.

David was willing to wrestle with Bathsheba's marital status because Satan's foothold was growing stronger. So the king had her delivered to him. Even her pregnancy proved no insurmountable problem. Satan quickly inspired David with a clever plan which would allow him to save face: Have her husband, Uriah, sent back home from war for an amorous visit with his wife so that the king's paternity would never be suspected. David tried this approach, but unfortunately for him, Uriah was a committed soldier of strong character. Refusing to indulge himself in sexual pleasures while his comrades were still roughing it, Uriah never even went home.

David panicked. But Satan, having established a new stronghold in this great man of God, could plant a thought so evil that it would never have taken root before: secretly order Joab, his commander, to send Uriah to the front line of battle so that he would be killed; then quickly marry Bathsheba so that her pregnancy would seem legitimate.

All this transpired according to plan. Because he had first granted Satan a secure foothold, David ended up breaking four of the Ten Commandments: those prohibiting murder, adultery, lying, and coveting. For his descent into such serious sin, God allowed Bathsheba's illegitimate child to die.

FOUR MENTAL STRONGHOLDS

Just as in David's time, today's foothold carries all the promise of becoming tomorrow's stronghold. The common spiritual struggles of the male species fall under four categories of mental strongholds that can be easily remembered as four s's: *self, success, silver, and sex.* We will consider the first three in the remainder of this chapter. Because men are so susceptible to self-deception in the fourth, we will examine issues surrounding sexual temptation in the following chapter.

Self. Self embraces everything related to personal comfort, including entertainment and recreation. We discussed some of these footholds in our portrait of the male warrior. Most of us are quick to conclude that we work hard (regardless of how hard we actually do work) and therefore deserve a certain amount of reward, rest, or pleasure. Yet the insistence on certain times, amounts, or styles of fun can assume the proportions of an unspoken right.

Suppose you enjoy eighteen holes of golf with your buddies every Saturday. Again, because you work long and hard during the five previous days, you feel you *deserve* this get-away. You cannot imagine a thing wrong with these six hours of harmless pleasure (and exercise, which every man needs, right?). And perhaps there is no problem.

But if you're married, your free time may not be as free as it once was. You need to maintain an open dialogue with your wife, as well as an open flow with God through prayer, about every aspect of your time, recreational or otherwise. After all, "You are not your own; you were bought at a price" (1 Corinthians 6:19-20). Because you belong to Christ, self has been dethroned.

Unfortunately, the self isn't very willing to step down from the throne. Due to the tendency of the flesh, in many cases complicated by years spent as a slave to sin before knowing Christ, the thought life lags behind the spiritual reality of the lordship of Christ. Ephesians 4:17-19 describes the process by which those separated from God naturally focus on their selves: "Gentiles... in the futility of their thinking... are darkened in their understanding and separated from the life of God because of the ignorance that is in them due to the hardening of their hearts. Having lost all sensitivity, they have given themselves over to sensuality so as to indulge in every kind of impurity, with a continual lust for more."

The alternative for those called by God is "to put off your old self, which is being corrupted by its deceitful desires" (Ephesians 4:22). Because you're dealing with desires, and deceitful ones at that, this involves no small amount of battle in the mind. Whether you're dealing with harmless desires, such as pursuit of a hobby, or harmful desires, such as drug use, you must face the stronghold of self and put it in its place. Just because you feel you have a right to something doesn't mean it *is* right. Eventually you can "be made new in the attitude of your minds" as you "put on the new self, created to be like God in true righteousness and holiness" (Ephesians 4:23-24).

Success. As we've seen in earlier chapters, success is a particularly important area for men because so much of our identity rests on what we accomplish. Many of us can even settle for making less than the biggest bucks as long as we're deemed successful in a respected profession, such as being a college professor.

One danger is wanting to look good in the eyes of man instead of the eyes of God. Jesus warns us: "Woe to you when all men speak well of you" (Luke 6:26). And in stronger language: "What is highly valued among men is detestable in God's sight" (Luke 16:15).

How many of us can embrace these words? I find it extremely difficult. It seems that a man is born and raised to become someone who will be spoken well of by other men—and this comes primarily through a successful career. Yet how many times have you read about a man who has worked so hard to build his business that he has lost his family? How many men do you know whose long hours on the job have brought on stress that leads to alcohol or drug addiction?

One man accepted a promotion, only to find that the extra hours demanded of him resulted in continual frustration. He came to despise those he worked with. He felt cheated because he was unable to see his family as much as he needed, and though he attended church, it was of little help.

"I feel divorced from anything spiritual," he said.

A lifetime focused on nothing higher than cultivating career advancements and the praise of others becomes a stronghold of idolatry—the love of humankind exceeding the love of God. Jesus commanded us to love others as we love ourselves.

Instead, we tend to practice a twisted version: Patronize others so they will revere us.

Silver. Just as nothing is inherently wrong with pleasure and recreation, or with success, money in itself is not sinful. But Scripture issues a strong warning about how we should regard it: "For the love of money is a root of all kinds of evil. Some people, eager for money, have wandered from the faith and pierced themselves with many griefs" (1 Timothy 6:10). Set your heart on money, and it's likely to lead you away from the faith, away from godliness.

The thought life is quite facile here, too. Just think how many day-to-day problems could be "solved" with more money: you could replace your four-wheel junk heap with a real car; you could tithe more easily; you would argue less with your wife over money if you had enough to satisfy all needs and wants. Haven't you ever entertained such thoughts when your checking account looked a lot slimmer than your stack of bills?

Of course, it doesn't take too many rides on life's merry-go-round to realize how fallacious such thoughts about money can be. The joy that comes with a new car doesn't last very long, until the moment that first painful scratch or dent marks it as merely mortal. And even new cars need repair soon enough. If your heart isn't right to begin with, tithing can become even harder with a higher income. Ten percent of a big paycheck is harder to part with than ten percent of a small paycheck. And likewise, arguments with your wife over how to spend thirty thousand a year could easily escalate if you had sixty thousand to spend. Household budgets are sort of like children: the problems only get bigger as they grow.

Jesus understood the futility of putting your trust in worldly wealth. He told a parable about a farmer who had a good crop—more than his barn would hold. His mind immediately raced ahead, and he decided he would tear down his barn and build bigger ones. He daydreamed about how he would say to himself, "You have plenty of good things laid up for many years. Take life easy; eat, drink and be merry" (Luke 12:19).

The farmer was losing this mental battle before he had ripped the first board from his old barn. Jesus explained the farmer's fatal flaw: "But God said to him, 'You fool! This very night your life will be demanded from you. Then who will get what you have prepared for yourself?' This is how it will be with anyone who stores up things for himself but is not rich toward God" (Luke 12:20-21).

FLEE AND FIGHT

First Timothy 6 instructs how to avoid the relentless, empty pursuit of money. The very same advice could be applied just as well to the self-serving pleasures money can buy and the success so often measured by income: "But you, man of God, flee from all this, and pursue righteousness, godliness, faith, love, endurance, and gentleness. Fight the good fight of the faith. Take hold of the eternal life to which you were called" (6:11-12).

Flee: In a situation of potential conflict, a person or an army hightails it in reverse when defeat appears to be imminent. You cannot expect to become too cozy with pleasure and money and still subject all your thoughts about them to Christ. "But if we have food and clothing, we will be content with that," recommends 1 Timothy 6:8.

Fight: In our flight from potential strongholds, we are to "pursue righteousness, godliness, faith, love, endurance, and gentleness." Be assured that Satan will hotly oppose you in your pursuit of the things of God. Be prepared to "fight the good fight of the faith" and to "take hold of the eternal life."

Eternal life is contrasted with the transient fluff of earthly life that attracts the flesh like a magnet, namely selfish pleasure, success, and silver. The more you set your mind on the eternal things of God, the less you'll be drawn to focus on the temporary things. Once those superficial elements capture your attention, they start to strut through your consciousness with thoughts that defy the lordship of Christ.

Satan wants to keep us focused on outward things, neglecting the precious inner life of Christ. Having fought the good fight of faith, the apostle Paul reminds us of the eternal perspective: "Though outwardly we are wasting away, yet inwardly we are being renewed day by day. For our light and momentary troubles are achieving for us an eternal glory that far outweighs them all. So we fix our eyes not on what is seen, but on what is unseen. For what is seen is temporary, but what is unseen is eternal" (2 Corinthians 4:16-18).

Don't be discouraged if the temptation of self, success, and silver continue to wage war in your mind. They should, in fact, seem to be more troublesome than in the past if you're really giving yourself over to be "renewed day by day" because you are stoking the conflict. So rejoice! That inner renewal is producing "an eternal glory that far outweighs" the weight of temptation. Just as exercise strengthens a muscle, your mind is being renewed in strength and purity, making you better equipped for winning the struggles of your thought life.

SEVEN

Sexual Sabotage

M ANY A SPEAKER on lust has asked this rhetorical question: what is man's biggest sex organ? Answer: the one that sits on top of his shoulders.

Your head comes equipped with a pair of eyes and a brain, the two elements vital to the lust process. With your eyes, you can scan the other half of the human race, the half you used to avoid when you were a little boy. It usually doesn't take long before you quit scanning and start fixating. Then the thought life takes over—visualizing, fantasizing, romanticizing. In peak form, the carnal nature seeks to immediately satisfy physical appetites which God designed to be satisfied only within the confines of a marital covenant.

Warfare of the mind requires you to be actively vigilant. A battle over lust that's lost in the mind amounts to sin even if nothing else transpires. Jesus wasn't exaggerating when he said, "Anyone who looks at a woman lustfully has already committed adultery with her in his heart" (Matthew 5:28). And once you grant Satan a foothold in this crucial area of sensuality, a stronghold will likely develop, which leads to even more sin, trouble, and heartache. What successful strategies can help us remain victorious in this battlefront?

NIP IT IN THE BUD

The admonition to "take captive every thought to make it obedient to Christ" certainly applies to lust (2 Corinthians 10:5). But because the sexual drive can be so strong, we do best when we can avoid having to spar with thoughts before getting them sufficiently under control. The warning against giving the devil a foothold has perhaps no more serious application than here.

Warfare is anything but static. Two opponents are constantly maneuvering, shifting forces, changing strategies, winning, or losing. Satan doesn't seek a foothold in your life just because he wants to chalk up a sin every now and then, the way World War II sailors painted an emblem on their battleship for every enemy plane they shot down. Satan wants to establish a stronghold that will bring you down to as much humiliation, ruin, and despair as possible, making forgiveness seem impossible, and thereby destroying your confidence as a man rooted in Christ.

James 1:14-15 summarizes Satan's system of destruction in the sensual realm: "Each one is tempted when he is carried away and enticed by his own lust. Then when lust has conceived, it gives birth to sin; and when sin is accomplished, it brings forth death" (NAS). Whether the lust revolves around sex or some other physical appetite, it certainly involves a bodily craving. But the warfare begins, and the outcome is largely determined, in the thought life. Unless errant thoughts are brought into subjection and examined as to whether or not they conform to the righteousness of Christ, they will carry you away, as James warned. How critical that we deal with temptation in its earliest stages.

A married man I know travels a few times a year to conduct sales in Central and South American countries. He occasionally meets with representatives whose hospitality may be excessive to the point of harm. "Lots of times folks want to take you and show you the town," he said. One representative handed him the telephone number of a woman who would make his stay a memorable one. This salesman turns down all such offers. And whenever he deals with female representatives (although rare in Latin cultures), he excuses himself from all invitations to a one-on-one meal.

Dr. James Dobson's Focus on the Family ministry maintains a similar safeguard. Staff policy prohibits a man and woman from going out of town together by themselves. Even though the likelihood of trouble may be minimal, the practice ensures that there will be no appearance of evil, which in itself is important for the reputation of any man or woman, single or married. And when we avoid the appearance of impropriety, we also go a long way toward eliminating the potential for serious sin.

The importance of appearances highlights another basic principle of sexual sabotage: while it takes two to tango, it takes only one to blab. Your own strength to resist sexual temptation, or your basic disinterest in a certain woman, does not provide a sufficient defense in compromising situations. Satan, ever scheming, cares little about attacking you where you are strong. He's probing for the soft spot, an opportunity to capitalize on the element of surprise.

We read about one such victim of a sneak attack in Genesis 39. Joseph was already riding the jet stream of the miraculous. As a youth, his dreams had depicted him as being exalted over his eleven brothers. They responded to the news by selling Joseph into slavery in Egypt, where he quickly became head of the household of Potiphar, the captain of Pharoah's guard. God blessed Joseph in everything he did.

Without any apparent provocation, Potiphar's wife tried to seduce the comely Hebrew. Even though Joseph flatly refused, she continued her advances for many days. Finally, the frustrated woman grabbed Joseph's cloak as he ran from one of her attempts at seduction. In anger, she turned the story upside down, claiming that Joseph had attacked her, leaving his cloak as he fled from her screams. For all of Joseph's integrity, he still landed in prison.

Being no more than a slave in charge of a household, perhaps Joseph could have done nothing more to escape the woman of the house. But the rest of us can almost always avoid being trapped in such a pressure cooker long before the heat gets turned on. It's often a matter of taking thoughts captive—perhaps not thoughts of lust, but naïve or self-deceptive thoughts. "I can handle this situation." Or "I've known her for years; she would never resort to anything crazy." Or "I'm happily married and I've never been seriously attracted to another woman." These kinds of smug thoughts can become a foothold from which Satan gains a fatal stronghold.

A SLIPPERY SLOPE

Satan's cleverness in establishing a foothold for sexual sin can be clearly seen among men in full-time ministry, where the vast majority of affairs stem from counseling situations. Though most of us work in secular jobs, we can still learn from their experience. Wise ministers avoid being alone with a woman, no matter how desperate the situation. It is far too easy for the "Christian" hug, the compassionate touch extended to a hurting person, to become directly personal, and then romantic and sexual.

How shrewd Satan can be! Consider the outward circumstances of such a counseling situation. Both people involved are Christians. At least one of them has even devoted his life to full-time ministry. They're meeting for a noble cause, perhaps to help restore the woman's marriage. Neither one comes with any intention of adultery. Yet in a situation seemingly dripping with righteousness, this man and woman of God could easily fall headlong into moral failure, complicating existing problems and creating new ones.

Such vulnerability demonstrates the marvelous, though dangerous blend of body, soul, and spirit which makes up a human being. As we discussed earlier, the Word of God is like a sharp sword, dividing soul and spirit (Hebrews 4:12). It can help separate the thoughts and desires that stem from the soul—the seat of will and emotion—from the pure thoughts and the perfect will of God that flow from the spirit. Only God's Word provides ultimate truth and clarity. Basing our counsel and behavior on this firm foundation makes us capable of sorting out the sometimes murky details in man's inner recesses.

Hebrews 4:12 goes on to say that God's Word "judges the thoughts and attitudes of the heart." Being proud and self-sufficient creatures, we men much prefer to be our own judges. We tend to give high marks to our self-discipline and moral fiber. Yet we too often fall victim to our own over-estimation. We fail to let God divide soul from spirit.

Though the following incident happened to a woman, men are just as susceptible to dangerous entanglements of soul and spirit. The woman was having an affair and sought counsel from some Christians. Through their advice, she understood that she needed to break off the affair, but insisted on maintaining some contact with the man by telephone or letter. She continued to resist a complete severing of the relationship and eventually moved away. Longing for her lost love and not wanting to hurt him, this woman could not escape the inner turmoil. Even the wise counsel she had sought, based on the Word of God, couldn't penetrate her emotional resistance. Her confused soul would not mesh with the righteous quickening of her spirit.

Don't underestimate the malleability of the soul. Even men outside of full-time ministry need to avoid becoming intimate confidants of women who are troubled. Likewise, we must avoid seeking a female friend to privately hear our own personal problems. The fact that neither of you felt attracted to each other at first matters not a whit. A few times of personal sharing usually form strong bonds that can prove difficult to break.

The volatility of potential sexual encounters, particularly in the context of harassment in the workplace, has become a major issue even outside of the Christian arena. On one hand, sinful men have more than ample opportunity to say and do something sexual which is clearly wrong. On the other hand, women may exaggerate, or even fabricate incidents of sexual harassment, with incalculable harm to reputations and legal costs to the employer. The problem is so widespread, and sometimes so hard to define, that companies have begun devoting considerable training to guard against abuse and the appearance of abuse.

You need to beware, also, of situations that are much more of an open assault, and by the element of surprise can achieve what would not otherwise be possible.

Christian author Jerry Jenkins, for example, tells about the time in a strange city when he was solicited by a prostitute. Caught off guard, he was nervous.

"No, thank you," he said. Jenkins apologized for having to turn her down, saying he hoped she wasn't offended.

Later on he mused to himself: *While the woman may have been looking only to take away my cash, Satan was looking to take away my integrity and ruin my marriage. And there I was, being polite.*

For Jenkins, like many of us, doing business with a hooker holds no more allure than going swimming at a water treatment plant. I'm not suggesting that you simply shrug off the potential danger of such temptations. Many men obviously have a weakness for purchased sex with anonymous women. Every man with a normal sex drive is vulnerable to sexual temptation, given the right circumstances, and Satan is sly enough to arrange customized circumstances sooner or later.

Any married man can testify that a wedding ring and a Christian marriage do not ward off temptations or lustful thoughts. Some men chalk up minor excursions as good-natured fun, such as gawking at professional football cheerleaders on television, or seeing how far they can flirt without getting flak from their wives. The issue is much more serious. We are caught up in a life and death struggle. Satan's nature is to kill and destroy. If he can destroy the integrity and self-esteem of a man with a family through adultery, he may score a package deal: possibly divorce, and all its fallout of emotional distress for both spouses and the children, often with lifelong consequences.

BACK FROM THE BRINK

It was his marriage, the man said. His wife had been poking around with questions. With this explanation, a man we'll call Tom approached a pastor and professional counselor for help. By the third visit, the pastor felt he had established enough trust to probe a little deeper. He suspected that Tom's "marriage" problem was actually an adultery problem.

"Are you having an affair?" he asked.

"Yes," admitted Tom. "I don't know why, but with the stress at work, and my wife complaining all the time, I began to notice this other woman who seemed to have an interest in me."

Tom's wife complained that he was not being an effective father and husband—a criticism which held a lot of truth. Tom should have been humbled. Instead, he fumbled.

We men—for all our physical might, all our business accomplishments, all our athletic records, all our imagined sexual prowess, all the strut and swagger we learn so well as teenagers and polish into adulthood—break quite easily. As we saw in the portrait of a male warrior, our brittleness has its roots in how we perceive ourselves. We're too often wallowing in an identity crisis that we can't—or won't—even talk about. And in an attempt to compensate, we often do foolish things.

Tom exhibited at least a few cracks in his manly facade. His complaint of "stress" at work is another way of saying failure, at least in part. Many men like to see themselves as masters of what they get paid for; the only problem they care to admit about their jobs is that they're not being paid enough.

Tom's wife had confronted him about his failures at home. Though some men clearly rank their family roles below that of provider, even the workaholic at least wants to think he's a caring father and an attentive husband. And no one, male or female, warms up to repeated criticism about anything—especially from someone as close as his or her spouse. One tempting outlet is to find a lover who offers companionship instead of criticism.

In fact, when it comes to lust, the vulnerable area for married men is not so much physical beauty. Sure, stunning looks will turn heads. Yet counselors will tell you that looks and sex for its own sake are not typically the first culprits to drive a wedge between a man and his wife. Driven by insecurity, some kind of emotional attachment most often paves the way into an adulterous relationship.

No man ever escapes the temptations to disengage his mind from reality and indulge in fantasizing. If you're married, rest assured that Satan will test your resolve to remain faithful when hard times hit. Knowing that God alone can be your source of security, you need to avoid complacency and stay alert to the wiles of the one who seeks to destroy you.

A turning point with Tom was getting him to confess his infidelity to his wife. The confession certainly wasn't all one-sided. His wife had to come to grips with her contribution to their problems as well. Though her unkind criticism of her husband in no way excused his adultery, admitting her role in hurting the marriage played an integral part of the restoration process.

Tom's confession to his wife and to God was followed by basic Christian therapy. He was guided into a personal Bible study to identify who he is in Christ and who Christ is in him. Tom came to realize that Christ is the sufficiency that makes him acceptable. He was also incorporated into regular church fellowship, an important source of strength and support.

Being around other Christians who accept us for who we are—warts, scars, habits, burps, and all—helps us to believe that God accepts us unconditionally. Unconditional love doesn't mean that our faults are beyond change, but that all of us are co-travelers on a journey in which God is at work to change us day by day.

STRATEGIES IN SEXUALITY

If you're married, the best overall strategy in guarding your thought life against lust is to build and maintain a strong marriage. Of course, entire books are written on this subject, and a complete marriage and sexuality primer is beyond the scope of this one. But I would like to offer several pointers which are specific to spiritual warfare, generally useful to married men and in some cases single men. These principles can help you to develop a state of mind and a discipline of spirit better equipped to expose, capture, and dispose of carnal and satanic thoughts.

Appreciate the natural beauty of women as part of God's creation. You don't need to feel guilty just because you noticed that a woman is attractive. Satan would love for pangs of accusation to grip you every time you see a pretty woman. If the guilt is strong enough, it will paralyze you, rendering you ineffective for the real spiritual battles that need to be fought. You may even feel so defeated that you consider a proper stance toward lust hopeless, and thereby give yourself over to whatever pathetic thoughts and practices your lust will lead you to.

Learn to draw the line. James 1 warns of being carried away with lust, so don't give your imagination an open-ended flight voucher. The same passage also tells us that lust has the ability to conceive. Don't let your thoughts about another woman give birth to something more substantive. No mental undressing. No comparisons with your wife. No time-traveling to past sexual experiences.

Do not underestimate Satan's cleverness. In not giving the enemy a foothold, continually remind yourself that Satan will gladly use the cross to dig his first little foxhole on your turf. You face an extremely shrewd adversary. I agree with those who believe that the more mature a Christian is, the more sophisticated Satan's approach.

Paul warns that "Satan himself masquerades as an angel of light. It is not surprising, then, if his servants masquerade as servants of righteousness" (2 Corinthians 11:14-15). One recent sexual scandal germinated in a large, successful church. Because of their maturity and position, the leaders claimed that God had granted them permission to express "Christian" love in a sexual way with women to whom they were not married. When their immoral behavior came to light, it caused untold damage to several individuals, to the church, and to the name of Christ.

I used to think that I had little problem with lust. Then I became aware of a recurring subject of mental speculation: *If my wife died unexpectedly, I would be free to marry. Who would she be? Let's see, who's available? Who looks good? I wonder what things would be like with —* ? When I shared my thoughts with other men, I discovered I wasn't alone.

Satan's cleverness in that situation was finding a presumption based on legitimate moral ground. The problem lies in the "what if," the speculation. The 2 Corinthians 10:4-5 passage on spiritual warfare tells us that speculation can often be completely opposed to God: "The weapons of our warfare are not of the flesh, but divinely powerful for the destruction of fortresses. We are destroying speculations and every lofty thing raised up against the knowledge of God, and we are taking every thought captive to the obedience of Christ" (NAS).

You can assume that any speculative thought that points toward sexual pleasure with someone other than your wife, no matter how legitimate the premises, needs to be taken captive and left in the dungeon. If Satan cannot gain a foothold through the back door, he's smooth enough to come right in through the front door, masquerading as an angel of light.

To say no to impurity, say yes to purity. God certainly calls married men to purity, but altogether abstaining from sexual behavior provides special challenges for single men—some of whom are at an age when their bodies are awash in hormones. Meanwhile, they see total sexual freedom being celebrated in most aspects of popular media. No matter how many peers they have at their church, these men remain outgunned in the war for moral purity.

"It's not just a matter of saying 'no' more emphatically," said a youth pastor. That amounts to no more than a "hopeless shortcut." Instead of denial, try affirmation. Fill your thought life with positive truth—like Scripture and Christian reading—the fodder that fuels the kind of godly life to which you aspire. R. Kent Hughes, in *Disciplines of a Godly Man*, observes that Christian literature is full of the advice of those who have struggled with every spiritual battle faced by modern man. To deny ourselves the precious wealth of what they discovered is "to embrace spiritual anorexia."[1]

Wise counsel alone cannot fill our minds with the ways of God. We also need heavenly oriented thoughts in general to produce the strength of character necessary to diminish thoughts of impurity. As Paul commands in Philippians 4:8: "Whatever is right, whatever is pure, whatever is lovely, whatever is admirable—if anything is excellent or praiseworthy—think about such things."

The thought life need not be a completely exposed battlefield, undefended against whatever bombs and missiles the enemy wants to hurl our way. We can take specific steps to defend our minds, just as we can launch offensives. After determining what thoughts are governed by our will, we can figure out what's pleasing to God, and read about and think about such things.

If you're married, talk about your courtship and continue to court. Many men and women have a strong romantic streak that doesn't just wither after the wedding. We may still long to experience the intoxication of flirtation and courtship—a strong ego need that's common after years of marriage. Rather than fantasizing about someone new, married men can continue through word and deed to relive that early stage of romance they shared with their wives.

Failure to continue courtship is one of the biggest problems in virtually every marriage. Any number of reasons can be given: lack of desire on the part of one or both partners; the failure to see the importance of romance; the lack of time or energy due to demands of children and jobs. The imperative to fight this drift from romancers to roommates is a key part of building any marriage. The spiritual dimension becomes apparent when you realize that marriage mirrors the union of Christ and his church. Satan wants to destroy anything that reflects the true nature of Christ or his body, the church.

Remind each other of your love and your wedding vows. The world of business is full of contracts. Don't neglect the most important contract, or covenant, you've made—the one with your wife. Unlike some business contracts, your marriage vows were not peppered with options, escape clauses, and fine print. The lifelong commitment of marriage also mirrors the steadfast love of God.

Talk about your problems, but not in the context of divorce. Communication between spouses is one of the greatest defensive weapons in marriage. Communication brings light, and light routs the darkness, upon which Satan depends to weave his webs of deceit and destruction. As much as possible, frame your discussion of problems in a way that divorce is not an option. The more you talk about something as a real possibility, the more possible it becomes. Talk breeds thoughts, and thoughts pertaining to divorce tend to lead in only one direction. Take captive such speculations. Do away with them. Refocus yourself on preserving your commitment to a lifelong covenant.

Don't be deceived by Satan's attractive presentation of divorce. We all have friends or relatives who have separated or divorced. Don't kid yourself. The rumored benefits of divorce, the private horror stories of someone who has endured a miserable marriage, or the joyful recovery of a divorced spouse, can begin to influence you.

Whenever your marriage is under stress, Satan will put a coat of shiny enamel over the tragedy of divorce. He may highlight someone who has remarried with apparent success, while hiding the difficulties that lie behind that facade or the pain of the transition for the divorced partner. He will keep under wraps the emotional turmoil, the lasting traumas, the behavioral problems that accompany the partners and children of most divorces. He will not give you a glimpse of the victorious testimony that a couple could have had if they had labored through counseling, prayer, and self-denial to rebuild their relationship on the rock of Christ.

Satan will practice this deception with all his might. He's more than willing to conduct guerilla warfare, picking off people and families one by one. Your enemy wants you to make every tactical mistake you possibly can, and divorce is one of the most serious battlefield errors you can make.

"May you rejoice in the wife of your youth" (Proverbs 5:18). Good advice. Neither you nor your wife can escape the physical aspects of the aging process, but that doesn't mean you should quietly moan while it defeats you over the years.

My wife complains about the unfairness of the movies, where men in their forties and fifties and sixties are still considered sexy enough to be paired with nubile women young enough to be their daughters, if not their granddaughters. She's right. Life isn't fair, nor is it Hollywood. As you move through the second half of your life, you may or may not acquire the debonair look of an elderly Sean Connery. But one thing remains certain: No fountain of youth will transport your wife back to the appearance of her twenties.

Nor should you desire such a marvel. Life is a journey, and so is marriage. A marriage can turn dull long before the wrinkles cross a woman's face. The challenge is to continually build the relationship with shared experiences, new depths of communication, and a sense of being jointly called in Christ, even if neither of you has a particularly visible ministry.

A man who is doing his part to lead a growing, thriving marriage can honestly rejoice in the wife of his youth. He remains glad that he chose her. The early infatuation with her physical beauty and personal charms has not so much disappeared as it has evolved into something deeper and more comprehensive. Against such a husband, Satan cannot gain a foothold through thoughts of younger women or thoughts of a wife's physical changes. That's because the husband, with God's help, has built a stronghold of righteousness that cannot easily be penetrated.

Rest in your perfection in Christ. Are you single, wishing only that you had a Christian wife? Are you married, disappointed that marriage has not proven to be as fulfilling as you had hoped? At the risk of sounding trite and superficial, you can be "complete in Christ" (Colossians 1:28) even in the midst of physical and emotional isolation.

However strongly you feel an emptiness or a lack in your life, abiding in Christ provides the essentials. Disappointments occur in all human relationships—whether in friendship, marriage, or other familial ties. Selfish motives take over. Love waxes and wanes. The most successful, intimate relationship you could imagine remains but a shadow of the communion God desires to have with you.

As far as we know, the apostle Paul was a single man, yet his writings show no trace of regret or self-pity because of his celibacy. Was he born with this attitude? No. He admits he had to *learn* certain lessons by following God and fighting his own spiritual battles: "I know what it is to be in need, and I know what it is to have plenty. I have learned the secret of being content in any and every situation, whether well fed or hungry, whether living in plenty or in want" (Philippians 4:12-13). In the same spirit, one might add "whether single or married, whether happily or unhappily married."

The "secret of being content" is well worth learning. The old saying, "The grass is always greener," emphasizes how basic discontent is to human nature. Thoughts of discontent do not agree with obedience to Christ. You do well to take them captive. The best strategy for denying them entrance to your mind is to cultivate contentment with Christ. Spend time with God and his Word. Meditate on how good he has been to you, how much you have for which to be thankful. Such thoughts leave no room for discontent.

If you're keeping your thought life under control, regularly soliciting God's help to prevent the devil from gaining a foothold, you're well-equipped to fight on battlegrounds other than the one between your ears. In the next chapter, let's zero in on an area of spiritual warfare which married men face: the battle of leadership.

EIGHT

A Demotion to Leadership

W HEN YOU DECIDED TO MARRY that smiling woman who always seemed to enjoy holding your hand, did you foresee the spats you would have over what kind of car to buy? Did it ever occur to you that the feminine creature who laughed so heartily at all your jokes would be so... so unappreciative of the finer things in life, such as watching the Dallas Cowboys dismember the Philadelphia Eagles on a Sunday afternoon?

No. Of course not. You had visions of sugar plums dancing in your head: romantic evenings by the fireplace that exceeded your wildest dreams, the aroma of sizzling steaks wafting through the house as you came home from work each day, not to mention the full breakfasts she would gladly throw together every morning. And if you were both Christians, you may also have envisioned the simple, peaceful order of a woman submitting to her husband, just like it says somewhere in the Bible, just like she said she would in the wedding vows, in everything.

Everything? Well, time has a way of redefining certain words, words like "submission." Before marriage, your pastor probably warned you that there would be times when you and your wife would argue. He may even have used the word "fight," but you two lovebirds probably squeezed hands under the table and figured that you were the exception to the rule. The special love that you had for one another would somehow defuse those little misunderstandings before they became a full-blown "conversation with the flying plates," as the old song goes.

If you've been married for any length of time, you now know the truth: Conflict related to authority is part of marriage. If you're like me, you learned by honeymoon day two that there would occasionally be less than a consensus about the husband's decisions as esteemed head of the household.

Stalemates over submission do not negate this aspect of the marriage relationship, which springs from Scripture. God does, indeed, have something to say about a husband's role as head over his wife. We're talking about one of the few ways men can take on a major responsibility without first proving themselves faithful. It takes only two words: "I do."

Some men ignore this responsibility. Some embrace it and do their best to handle it as a faithful steward. Others zap it with their magic macho wand, turning it into a privilege which they proceed to abuse by dominating their wives physically or emotionally. But no man who jumps into marriage escapes the mantle of headship that comes with the territory.

Because of their nature and their opportunities to further God's kingdom, every man—whether married or single—should consider himself as a potential officer in God's army. We should be willing to lead and train others in his service as occasions arise. However, many of us would just as soon avoid one aspect of leadership. Jesus put it this way: "Whoever wants to be great among you must be your servant, and whoever wants to be first must be your slave—just as the Son of Man did not come to be served, but to serve, and to give his life as a ransom for many" (Matthew 20:26-28).

Having a servant's mentality means humility, and humility stands at odds with pride. As we press on to obey Jesus' teaching, we can expect direct opposition from Satan. He's the one who proudly exalted himself in the face of God and fell from heaven, the one who tempted Adam and Eve, saying, "You will be like God." As we learn to fulfill our role of family leadership, one of the best ways we can prepare ourselves to fight Satan is to embrace servanthood.

MY RIGHTS, YOUR RIGHTS

"I'm the boss of my family and my wife said I could say so." The laughter that always follows this statement seems tinged with nervousness. This muddled perspective on authority strikes too close to home for many men. A Christian husband may have a vague sense—perhaps from residual cultural norms or church teaching—that he is supposed to lead his family. Yet he may feel threatened by his wife, with whom he has never quite found that complementary relationship described in the Bible.

Both individuals in a marriage relationship are called to freely embrace servanthood. Scripture issues certain directives to the wife:

Wives, submit to your husbands as to the Lord. For the husband is the head of the wife as Christ is the head of the church, his body, of which he is the Savior. Now as the church submits to Christ, so also wives should submit to their husbands in everything.   **Ephesians 5:22-24**

Wives, in the same way be submissive to your husbands.
                                        1 Peter 3:1

Now I want you to realize that the head of every man is Christ, and the head of the woman is man, and the head of Christ is God.   **1 Corinthians 11:3**

The husband's responsibilities are outlined in Ephesians 5:

Husbands, love your wives, just as Christ loved the church and gave himself up for her to make her holy, cleansing her by the washing with water through the word, and to present her to himself as a radiant church, without stain or wrinkle or any other blemish, but holy and blameless. In this same way, husbands ought to love their wives as their own bodies. He who loves his wife loves himself. After all, no one ever hated his own body, but he feeds and cares for it, just as Christ does the church—for we are members of his body. "For this reason a man will leave his father and mother and be united to his wife, and the two will become one flesh." This is a profound mystery—but I am talking about Christ and the church. However, each one of you also must love his wife as he loves himself, and the wife must respect her husband.   Ephesians 5:25-33

As you can see, this last passage is a good bit longer than the earlier verses addressing the wife's responsibilities. On the other hand, the instructions to the man conclude with a parting shot to the wife: "respect your husband." Notice the absence of any escape clause. The couch-bound meathead still deserves respect from his Christian wife. At the same time, a husband should read all of Ephesians 5 as if the burden fell totally on his own broad shoulders. If you care for your wife in the way described, you will begin to cast a shadow into your home that resembles Christ. You will be worthy of respect.

One counselor believes that the husband's failure to assume his proper role can be found in about ninety percent of the Christian couples he counsels. And with the remaining ten percent, the marital problem involves not their relationship but some other issue which they jointly face, perhaps their children or their finances.

When a man fails to lead his wife spiritually and otherwise, she usually experiences ongoing frustration and stress. Some women in this situation will leave the marriage in order to reduce the tension. More often they won't leave, but neither will they be able to resolve their husband's inability or refusal to assume leadership in the home.

At that point, Satan has won a major battle. Husband and wife may remain Christian, but untold damage has been done. The nature of family is such that the whole is much greater than the sum of the parts. A malfunctioning marriage means not simply two unhappy people. It means that God has lost, at least in part, a productive training camp and mission school. A family growing in Christ has unlimited potential to touch dozens, if not hundreds of people, during their years together. Therefore, one challenge for married men is to make the offensive and defensive moves in time to avert emotional and physical separation and divorce.

Even though Paul was writing about husband-wife relationships in Ephesians 5, the same principles can be applied more broadly. Paul held up the model of a single man, Jesus, who cared for his church like a bridegroom caring for a bride. God has placed certain people in the lives of a single man, all in need of love and service. The single man should discern which of these needs he might be able to fulfill.

The highest plane of service falls within the mysterious bond between Christ and the church. Jesus is described in Ephesians 5 as loving, washing, sacrificing, presenting, feeding, and caring for the church. These activities can be grouped into three categories: love (loving and sacrificing), nurture (washing, feeding, and providing care), and purity (presenting a spotless bride who is the church).

These same actions can apply on the human level just as easily. Before returning to specific husband-wife matters, let's see how the challenges of walking in Christian love, nurture, and purity impact men and the church, and how the world, the flesh, and the devil wage war against it.

THE WAR ON LOVE

The fluttering stomach, the giddy lightness, the all-night conversations, the physical magnetism—these hallmarks of falling in love don't seem to fit the Ephesians 5 concept of love. Rather, Christians are pointed toward love in its pure form: self-sacrifice.

How would the majority of people rate giving up something for nothing for no reason other than to benefit someone else? The idea carries about as much leverage as Monopoly currency on the New York Stock Exchange. Everywhere one turns, the world, the flesh, and the devil have their pumps primed, ready to inflate self instead of allowing it to diminish through sacrifice. For example:

- Advertising keeps Americans in a feeding frenzy of materialism. Newer, bigger, faster, sleeker—you've got to have it. In fact, you should have had it yesterday. And yesterday's luxuries—a microwave oven, a television set, a second car—soon become today's necessities. The process stimulates people to discover more "needs" and to satisfy them. Materialism abhors the thought of self-denial. Society labels women as the shoppers, but men are just as susceptible to the lure of expensive goodies: clothes, cars, electronics, whatever. Most men have no more trouble than women in thinning out the wallet. As alert spiritual warriors, we must recognize that the world presents a relentless attack of materialism and comfort to keep us away from the prize of true Christian love.

- Sensuality, like materialism, has become an omnipresent part of modern Western culture, constantly tugging us away from the Christian ideal of self-sacrifice. It threatens us like a sprawling mine field, ready to destroy our personal integrity with one misstep. The barrage of sexual/sensual messages convinces more and more people, including Christians, that their physical self-gratification is paramount. The number of Christian men who indulge in pornography has grown to tragic proportions. Many of the men falling victim to its lure are married, yet their wives could never fulfill their sexual fantasies. Instead of viewing sexuality from a perspective of self-gratification, God calls married couples to focus on giving pleasure to one another.

- Just as it did in the downfall of Satan, pride plays a major role in leading men to inflate self rather than lay down their lives for others. Seeking desperately to establish their identities, men become preoccupied with magnifying themselves in their own eyes and in the eyes of others. Satan is quick to show Christian men ways they can exalt that self-image—any way except standing on the identity they have in Christ. Most red-blooded American males will use, abuse, and even trample upon any person who stands in the way of their unrelenting march toward power and prestige. The surest way they know to increase self is to belittle others around them.

THE WAR ON NURTURE

Ephesians 5 speaks of transition: the church, the bride of Christ, is being prepared to meet the Bridegroom at the end of earthly time. The more immediate comparison portrays the husband as nurturing his wife—cleansing, feeding, and caring for her.

Satan can be likened to a wayward teen-age boy looking for violent pranks, taking no greater joy than defiling something as precious as that nurturing process. Keenly aware of Satan's nature as one who destroys and kills, Jesus told a story about hindrances to the nurturing process—in this case, opposition to the seed of the gospel as soon as it's sown.

A farmer's seed landed on various surfaces. Some fell on the path, where the birds plucked it before it even took root. When the seed fell on rocky soil, the plants sprang up quickly; but the sun scorched them and they died because their roots were shallow. Other seed began to grow among thorns, which eventually choked out the plants. One final batch fell on good soil and yielded a fruitful crop. Jesus offered this interpretation:

> When anyone hears the message about the kingdom and does not understand it, the evil one comes and snatches away what was sown in his heart. This is the seed sown along the path. The one who received the seed that fell on rocky places is the man who hears the word and at once receives it with joy. But since he has no root, he lasts only a short time. When trouble or persecution comes because of the word, he quickly falls away. The one who received the seed that fell among the thorns is the man who hears the word, but the worries of this life and the deceitfulness of wealth choke it, making it unfruitful. But the one who received the seed that fell on good soil is the man who hears the word and understands it. He produces a crop, yielding a hundred, sixty or thirty times what was sown.   **Matthew 13:19-23**

Again, we see the world, the flesh, and the devil at work, in this case to cut short the fullness of what God intends. The "evil one," meaning Satan, will do all he can to steal truth as soon as it is dispensed, just as the birds plucked the seed off the path before it had a chance to take root. Satan, likewise, will make the Word of God seem dull; he will try to divert your attention in any kind of teaching situation; he will work to make you doubt the promises in Scripture.

The final two attacks in the parable could involve both the world and the devil. When a person has allowed the Word of God to take root in his life and then begins to catch some flak because of it, that new plant can be thwarted in its infancy. Routine anxieties and the false hopes attached to wealth are like thorns that kill the gospel plant as it moves toward maturity. The world and the devil promise, say, that a minor deception at work will bring a promotion, or they lead you to believe that if you only had X dollars more you would really be satisfied. Variations on the theme are endless.

Single men, you are immersed in a conflict that could keep you spiritual babes if it doesn't kill you outright. You really don't have to be accountable to anyone, except perhaps your employer. You could easily skip your Bible reading, your private time with the Lord, your participation in church. Who would know? Satan will whisper, "You've read all those Bible stories anyway. There's nothing new to be learned."

If you desire marriage, Satan will use that desire to derail your maturing process. When no marriage prospect is in sight, he can turn your longing into a major worry, as Jesus warned about. Or Satan may bring a perfect match into your life—perfect except that she doesn't share your faith. If you knowingly marry an unbeliever, you will probably encounter another difficulty about which Jesus warned: "trouble or persecution because of the word." Your marriage may or may not squeak along, but you will certainly be handicapped in your Christian growth.

Married men are also faced with an onslaught of "the worries of this life and the deceitfulness of wealth." Worries related to family alone are enough to topple a giant California redwood. So distracting are the duties of leading a family that a man bent on growing into Christian maturity does well if he chooses not to marry (1 Corinthians 7:1). Here's why: "An unmarried man is concerned about the Lord's affairs—how he can please the Lord. But a married man is concerned about the affairs of this world—how he can please his wife—and his interests are divided" (1 Corinthians 7:32-34).

As the one who conveys a child's first image of God's fatherhood, fathers are constantly challenged with nurturing their offspring at every age. Don't be misled by edited liturgies or hymns or Bibles that refer to God as mother, or alternately male and female. God revealed himself as Father in the Old and New Testament.

Neither did God's only begotten Son teach the great prayer as beginning, "Our Mother," or "Our Cosmic Power," or "Our Life Force." Jesus might have correctly said, "Oh God, who art in heaven," but he chose to stick with the revelation of the ages. The eternal spirit being who created the universe, whose ways are not our ways, whose thoughts are beyond our thoughts, nevertheless possesses the qualities of someone every human being can understand: a father.

In confusing the issue of God's identity, what is Satan's strategy? At first glance, we might assume that his chief desire is that children receive no image of God's fatherly nature. More and more people grow up in homes in which the father is absent or where both parents are unbelievers. Children in such circumstances are handicapped in their likelihood of coming to know God.

True to his nature of deception and half-truth, Satan busily attacks fathers in any way he can to ensure that children receive a distorted image of God's fatherhood. What is the best way that the father of lies can achieve his perverted goal? Through men who speak and act in ways contrary to godly standards.

Do you want to teach children that God contains a wise blend of mercy and judgment? Be consistent in your rules. Refrain from excessive leniency. Discipline consistently, appropriately, and promptly. Be open to mercy in circumstances that merit nothing more than a warning.

Do you want to teach children that God's promises are true? When you make a commitment, keep it. Psalm 15:4 says a righteous man is one "who keeps his oath even when it hurts." Christian seminar leader Bill Gothard speaks of adult men who still bear childhood wounds because a father reneged on a promise, such as a special outing.

Do you want to teach children that God is accessible, that he hears and responds to prayers? Be available. If you have children still living at home, carefully weigh every demand that takes you out of the home—that second job to earn a little extra money, those daily workouts at the health club, the civic group that wants you to work on its annual fund drive, the elder who wants you to teach a course at the church one evening a week.

When your children talk to you, give them your complete attention, including eye contact and if possible, physical contact. Of course, you also need to teach them things such as reasonable limits to a parent's time, the rudeness of interruptions, and the need of both parents to be alone occasionally. God, who nurtures all of us, will give you wisdom if you ask him.

THE WAR ON PURITY

Ephesians 5:27 explains that Jesus lived and died to present the church "to himself as a radiant church, without stain or wrinkle or any other blemish, but holy and blameless." In the same way, God calls all men to die to themselves for the sake of the church. We are to work and pray that the imperfect humanness that surrounds any organization will diminish and that Christlikeness may increase, unveiling a radiance that out-shines any counterfeit source of hope and help. A husband, desiring a pure wife, is to give up his life for her in the same way. He is called to embrace pain and inconvenience just as Christ embraced the lashes, the thorns, and the nails.

Satan will do anything within his power to throw black paint on the white garments of the church. One of his favorite battle tactics involves leading a minister into immorality of some kind and then having him exposed. The bigger the name, the better. Such news tends to discourage those who know God; those who don't often relish the hypocrisy, the confirmation that those goody-goodies were nothing more than slimy, silver-tongued serpents ("I told you about those preachers!"). When a leader is discredited, of course, he also brings down the repu-tation of any organization with which he's associated.

Ephesians 5:27 says that Christ gave himself to present a radiant *church,* not *churches.* If any crevice exists into which Satan can fit his wedge, he'll find it—gossip, doctrinal disputes, competition for growth, or hurt feelings. The more divided and discordant the body of Christ, the less it functions in a uni-fied way. The body is composed of many parts, but they work best when not maimed, anesthetized, or amputated.

Many different churches illuminated throughout a city

would shed a soft nighttime glow, but nothing distinguishable from a multitude of other urban lights. But the beacon from one church which consolidated all of the city's believers would pierce the sky like a search light. I don't mean to suggest that a church of thousands is better than a small church. Rather, it is the unity and level of faith among the believers—whether they belong to one church or one hundred—that can produce a glorious radiance which none can ignore.

The same principle applies to the husband-wife relationship. The transgressions of one party stain the reputations of both. Scripture tells us that the two became one in spirit the moment they were wed, yet worldly stresses constantly work to dissolve the glue that unites them. Just because Satan cannot lead a man or wife into divorce doesn't mean he can't fracture their unity.

Unbelievers may not be well-versed in Christianity, but this much they do know: that Christian marriage is supposed to be sacred and able to produce healthy, happy families for the most part. As long as Satan can spoil the purity of even one marriage with complacency, moral compromise, or divorce, he's succeeded in turning down the radiance of the church one more notch.

TIPPING THE SCALE

John the Baptist knew exactly where he stood when questioned about this new guy named Jesus who appeared to be stealing his ministry, even using baptism in his services: "He must increase, but I must decrease" (John 3:30, NAS). No identity problem here. John held what many men today covet: a position of powerful influence. Yet he had been waiting for the day when he could begin to bow out.

Husband, how do you decrease? Ephesians 5 offers clear counsel: give yourself up for your wife, just as Christ did for the church. What specifically are you to give? Yourself, your life, time, conversation, sympathy, whatever it is she needs.

How did Christ decrease? Even though he was the Son of

God, he counted his life as deserving nothing. He didn't even have a home once he began his ministry. He suffered; he bled; he even sweated blood, a phenomenon which occurs under severe stress. The most innocent man who ever lived, Christ died like a criminal at the hands of people who themselves deserved death.

Christ exemplified Paul's exhortation in Philippians 2:3-4: "With humility of mind let each of you regard one another as more important than himself; do not merely look out for your own personal interests, but also for the interests of others." You'll find few greater challenges in Scripture. The husband who regards his wife's interests as more important than his own will not hesitate to go cruising the mall with her in order to provide a time of informal conversation or some added security in choosing clothes. He will be extremely cautious before taking a job that requires a lot of traveling, or before becoming involved with a time-consuming hobby such as golf. Why? Because he remembers that his wife's interests are *more* important than his, and that the loss of time will limit his ability to serve her needs.

The single man is called to the same humility of mind. Often with more discretionary time and money than a married man, he can be alert to the child in a single-parent family who needs time with a male role model. The unmarried man can eagerly give of his finances—even to the point where it hurts or perhaps seems illogical—because he isn't depriving a family of comforts or needs.

SPIRITUAL SOAP

Paul offers another key to fighting Satan, particularly in regard to the purity of the church and of wives: "to make her holy, cleansing her by the washing with water through the word" (Ephesians 5:26). Remember that Jesus compared himself to "living water" (John 7:38).

How can a wife, or an entire church, be washed in this

water? One way is *through the Word of God.* In the church, it must be preached, practiced, and honored. A husband, as head of his wife, has the same responsibility at home. He can read God's Word to his wife. He can use it in his counsel for her. He can incorporate it in his prayer for her.

Dave found his wife sobbing one night over their oldest son. Months had passed since the teenager had left home, and he still rejected the God his parents had embraced and tried to teach at home. "I asked the Lord to give me a Scripture that would be an encouragement and comfort to her," Dave told me. "I did this without any deep conviction I would get anything."

Yet almost immediately, he felt sure that God wanted him to look at Jeremiah 31:17, though he had no idea what the verse concerned. He soon found out that it was God's word of comfort through the prophet, using the imagery of Jacob's wife Rachel, who was "weeping for her children and refusing to be comforted, because her children are no more" (Jeremiah 31:15). The following verse said: "'So there is hope for your future,' declares the Lord. 'Your children will return to their own land.'" That passage provided immense comfort for Dave's wife, as well as for him, as they faced the pain of a child who rejects God.

Scripture applied in such a way actually performs a cleansing function. Not that the husband forgives sin—God still holds that franchise. But a woman's fears and insecurities can be scoured away by the "washing with water through the word." Let's take a closer look at the claims God makes on his Word.

- God promises prosperity and success to those who meditate on his Word *and* act upon it. (Joshua 1:8)

- God's Word makes simple people wise. (Psalm 19:7)

- God's Word enables a man to keep his way pure. (Psalm 119:9)

- God's Word stands true eternally. (Isaiah 40:8)

- God's Word is spirit and life. (John 6:63)
- God's Word helps you build faith. (Romans 10:17)
- God's Word is like a spiritual sword, our best offensive weapon in spiritual warfare. (Ephesians 6:17)
- God's Word can act quickly and powerfully. (Hebrews 4:12)
- God's Word helps us distinguish between emotional thoughts and ones prompted by God. (Hebrews 4:12)

God has given us such a wonderful tool in the Bible, one we often take for granted. It goes a long way toward keeping your own life on a path of constant spiritual maturity. If you're married, God's Word also helps you to nurture, love, and purify your wife.

The responsibilities of leading a family are so overwhelming that's it's a wonder any man ever marries. Perhaps God allows our eyes to be blinded by love so that we won't walk down the aisle quaking with fear. Every married man has much to learn about self-sacrificing leadership, lessons which become all the more difficult in the midst of Satan's incessant attacks on family life. But by the grace of God, you can be rich soil for the seed of God's Word of abundant life as long as you remember what growth in the kingdom of heaven means: You must decrease as Christ increases.

Even though Jesus never married, he provided the perfect role model of how to combine manly servanthood and leadership. While he didn't hesitate to expel the vendors who defiled the temple, neither did he shrink back from embracing a child or speaking tenderly to a woman lost in sin. Let's go on to examine in greater detail how Jesus handled one of his most intense moments of spiritual warfare.

NINE

Forging a New Identity

C AN YOU IMAGINE an eyeball-to-eyeball encounter with the very embodiment of all evil? I don't mean getting splattered with obscenities by your boss, or being taken hostage by a deranged serial killer. I have in mind a situation of even greater intensity.

Picture a man who has just spent forty days fasting and praying in the desert. His beard cannot hide the jutting bones of his drawn face. Spiritually, he's charged. Physically, he's depleted. And he's just run into someone who would love to see this sun-baked hermit fatten up his gaunt rib cage by taking advantage of an all-the-bread-you-can-eat offer. This offer, however, requires a very special payment.

You may recognize these two characters as Jesus and Satan. Matthew 4 omits a great deal about their meeting: what Jesus prayed about during those forty days, in what form Satan appeared, and whether Jesus agonized over accepting the three offers laid before him by the tempter. It's not entirely clear why he chose to fast, but judging by the timing, his decision apparently was related to the beginning of his public ministry. Jesus must have had some inkling as to the unrelenting spiritual attacks by men and demons he was about to face. He wanted to be prepared for battle.

Matthew does state the three temptations and Jesus' concise, yet powerful refutations. You can find plenty of modern-day tales about the casting out of demons, complete with graphic details, but not one can top this confrontation for hard-core spiritual warfare: man against Satan, fighting for eternal stakes, no subtleties involved.

Before examining the individual temptations in the following two chapters, let's consider a broader application of this desert showdown. Though Jesus' ministry encompassed far more conflict than this single episode, it distills a crucial role he played: going before us as one who has been victorious over the same temptations we face, and who now intercedes on our behalf in the same way as an Old Testament high priest. Through studying the way Jesus resisted these temptations, we have much to learn about finding an anchor for male identity.

DELIVERING A DARE PACKAGE

Satan hurled three temptations at Jesus: to turn stones into bread; to fall from a tower and have angels save him; and to worship Satan in return for all the kingdoms of the world. In the way he phrased two of those three come-ons, Satan revealed his fondness for chipping away at a person's faith: "*If* you are the Son of God...."

Regardless of the degree of your spiritual maturity, or the amount of success you've had, Satan can always find some sensitive area to question, knowing you will listen. Because so many men have trouble finding a secure identity, Satan's calling card frequently questions a man's worth:

- "If you really are a good father, would your children be repeating those nasty words they learned on the school bus?"
- "If you really are a Christian man, would your head keep turning to glance at every woman who walks into the restaurant?"
- "If you really are a good husband, would you have snapped at your wife like you did on the way to church?"

- "If you really were a good steward over your finances, wouldn't you have more money to give the church?"

In the Matthew 4 passage, the Greek word commonly translated as "if" is more accurately rendered "since." For example, "*Since* you are the Son of God, why don't you use your special powers and do this or that." Satan uses this same tactic of presumption as a favorite back-door way to erode our own spiritual identity. "Since you know God will forgive you when you repent later, why don't you go ahead and rent a tape of that racy movie you've heard about?" Or "Since you've been working a lot on that upcoming church program, why don't you give yourself a break from doing your family devotional?"

Satan apparently knew he couldn't convince Jesus to doubt his own divinity, but his chances are much greater in persuading us to doubt *our* worth as sons of God. One way Satan accomplishes this is through the facile use of half-truth, as I discussed earlier. By using snippets of truth, the father of lies is able to draw us in on his terms. And herein lies one of the greatest dangers we face: allowing Satan to choose the stage for warfare. He offers a standing invitation to the valley of destruction, where he holds the high ground so that we will not be able to maneuver amid the flying arrows, spears, and rocks.

A FUTILE DEFENSE

Suppose you engage Satan on the battleground of your failure as a mature Christian to read the Bible and pray daily. Now you will not actually hear voices, and you may not be conscious of any sort of running dialogue, but this is the kind of demoralizing quagmire that you, as a shrewd soldier, want to avoid:

Satan: "You missed your prayer time again this morning."

You: "I know. But I was up late last night—and hey, it was a meeting to plan the church's men's retreat. That must count for...."

Satan: "Oh, come on. You hardly paid attention. The whole time you kept sneaking looks at your watch to see if you'd get home in time to catch the end of that TV movie."

You: "Well, I would have done it this morning, but I had to get to work in time for an early meeting. Besides, I read the Bible the day before. And I'm going to be sure not to miss tomorrow."

Satan: "I see. Two out of three's good enough for God, huh? You think being a part-time Christian is okay? Is that how much you love God?"

You: "God's not into counting like that. Anyway, I'm doing a lot more than I used to."

Satan: "Oh, that's sweet. Your little pittance of an effort is more than the absolute nothing you used to do. I'm sure God is impressed. How long ago did you hear that guy talking about how much it meant for him to get into his 'prayer closet'—isn't that what he called it?—every morning, and how he just didn't feel complete if he missed a day, and you promised your dear Lord that you would do the same. And then what happened? You started...."

You: "I know, I know...."

Satan: "And then that Bible study your men's group went through—remember all the talk about that verse: 'I have hidden your word in my heart that I might not sin against you'? And you were right in there, promising with the rest of your friends to memorize Scripture. So how much have you memorized lately? Sounds like that word is hidden in your stony old heart so well you couldn't dislodge it with a jackhammer."

And so it goes. The more you try to swim out of this vicious whirlpool by defending yourself, the further the vortex sucks you down. Why? Because none of us can mount a credible defense of ourselves and our performance. We sin. We fall short even when we don't sin. When our short memories allow some of our specific transgressions and general failings to fade away, the accuser loves to fill in the gaps.

Jesus had no failures to worry about. Nonetheless, he didn't bother to engage Satan by talking directly about the temptations. While forty days of fasting had rendered him extremely weak physically and looking like anything but a king, Jesus did not seem to feel insecure in his role. He didn't have to show off by working a miracle with the stones; he didn't seek the glamorous, powerful identity that would have come with rulership over the world's kingdoms.

Instead, Jesus proved the old saying that the best defense is a good offense. Citing Scripture, he fired back with truth that surpassed the superficial diversions Satan dangled before him. We need to employ the same offense in our spiritual battles by countering the truth of our failures with higher truths: who we are in Christ, the power he holds over Satan, and the reality of divine forgiveness.

TEMPTED IN ALL THINGS

One of the modern characters bequeathed to us by Hollywood is the Terminator, a virtually indestructible robot from the future. Once he's been programmed for a mission, no number of bullets can stop him. Burn off his fake flesh, and the high-tech skeleton keeps trudging along.

Some men perceive Jesus as so saintly that they often fail to think of him as a real man. They faintly picture him as a divine Terminator wearing sandals and a weak smile, trudging unswervingly toward his appointment with Calvary. The enemy arrows and flame-throwers never leave a scar. The post-desert temptations from Satan? No big deal. Like gnats buzzing around an elephant.

Satan employs this disinformation campaign to confuse the enemy troops, to persuade us that our leader was something that he wasn't. Jesus has always been the Son of God. When he made his brief tour of earth, he retained that divinity and became fully human at the same time. Jesus was a man in every sense that we are. While he never sinned, the Son of Man nevertheless was "tempted in every way, just as we are" (Hebrews 4:15). Jesus can help us resist temptation because he himself endured the same struggles.

As we saw in our discussion of enemy tactics, the Greek word translated here as "tempted" could also be "tested." If a man feels tempted to fantasize about a female teller he sees every week in the bank, he has a choice. The choice he makes determines whether he passes the test. God will permit us to endure various circumstances to test us, to see what's inside. But Satan is the tempter, the one who entices us to commit evil.

We men are almost cursed with having to continually prove ourselves, of passing test after test—often of our own making. We believe there's an identity out there, somewhere, if we can just nail it. This search for an identity shows up at every age. As children, we have to hold our own on the playground. As preteens, we jockey for any kind of sports success we can find. As teenagers, we try to discover that nebulous mix of being tough and cool that will make us attractive to girls. In college, we bounce around between majors and career ideas trying to figure out what society deems worthwhile. Once we settle into something as adults, we have to keep getting the promotion or the new job that puts a new coat of varnish on our name.

Testing, then, is part of our life and our nature. As much angst as we face in our journey from cradle to grave, this testing can also provide a little excitement here and there. I remember reading about the young owner of a computer company who despised waiting in airports for his flights to leave. As a man who enjoyed living on the edge, he began timing his departure for the airport later and later. On more than one occasion, he got tied up in traffic at or near the airport and had to sprint from the cab. This impatient traveler always made it to the gate on time, passing his self-imposed test. But he was no fail-proof Terminator. Neither are you, whether the challenges you face are physical or spiritual.

HIGH PRIEST AND ADVOCATE

Jesus was tempted not just after his fast, but throughout his life. Hebrews 2:17-18 tells us the reason: "He had to be made like his brothers in every way, in order that he might become a merciful and faithful high priest in service to God, and that he might make atonement for the sins of the people. Because he himself suffered when he was tempted, he is able to help those who are being tempted."

How does a "high priest" function in the courts of heaven? If you have accepted Christ and continue to repent of sins as you fall, you have a pre-paid legal service. Your attorney sits at the judge's right hand, holding much more clout than the prosecuting attorney. Jesus came to earth as a man to live and die as a sacrifice for our sins; in so doing, he fully qualified for the role of high priest. The fines you should receive for running spiritual red lights, Jesus has already paid through his death. The tests you face, he has passed. The evil that beckons to you, he has looked squarely in the eye and rejected. Through the ongoing dialogue of prayer, Jesus is willing—eager, actually —to help you through every trial.

You may be able to draw upon your personal store of self-discipline or self-sufficiency to get you through a few tests, biting your tongue to curb certain words that seem to capture your anger, for instance. But sooner or later, if the words don't squeeze their way through your clenched teeth, the vileness and anger will manifest themselves in other ways.

We need to call on our advocate for help sooner than later. Not only does Jesus plead our case when we need forgiveness, but he would rather help us achieve victory that will cut sin off at the pass. I'm convinced that many times the only thing that separates success from failure is whether or not we ask God's help. Jesus, who at a point of dire physical weakness was tempted by Satan, can sympathize with what feels to you like insurmountable weakness.

Suppose you feel so high-strung from an exhausting day at work that there's no way your children, even on their best behavior, could escape the volcanic wrath just waiting to erupt. Before you arrive home, pray for endurance. Ask for patience. Readily confess your fragility; God already knows it. On behalf of everyone in your household, ask God to defuse potentially explosive incidents, all the while knowing you must be prepared, with self-control, for the worst. Ask for a fresh infilling of his Holy Spirit to rise above your own self-centeredness and be the kind of husband and father God intends you to be. Preparation can make all the difference in how you respond to a test, and the strength with which you face Satan's temptation.

Of course, sometimes you feel so flushed with anger and moodiness that change seems hopeless, at least for the rest of the day. Satan deftly suggests that it would be pointless to dabble in any of that religious stuff until the storm has passed. His analysis usually feels right on. But don't listen. Your high priest will intercede on your behalf no matter how badly you're botching the battle, or how unfair the day's events have been.

In other words, God delights in pouring out his strength where you are weak. Paul discovered this marvelous reality: "I delight in weaknesses, in insults, in hardships, in persecutions, in difficulties. For when I am weak, then I am strong" (2 Corinthians 12:10). Whether your weakness is anger or something else, God is eager to give an emergency infusion of his strength.

Many times the turning point in passing a test comes when you pause for a conference with your high priest. This sounds like the easy, obvious thing to do when you're outside the heat of battle. But in the thick of it, Satan will do everything to delete that option from your consciousness. You'll be left with your emotions and your very fallible reason as the only guides.

Yet the more you discipline yourself to open up to God, the more of a habit it becomes. Suppose you bring before God a temptation to hide that little bit of outside income when tax time rolls around. Immediately, you've gained a major advantage. The more you talk to God about a temptation, the more the allure lessens. For one thing, you're inviting in a wise outside party of much higher rank. No one wants to be caught in the act by their superior. For another, God can assure you that he will honor your honesty, and that he will meet your financial needs even though no apparent provision is on the horizon.

WHERE REAL STRENGTH LIES

When are we weak? The truth is, we're weak all the time. Weak in the sense that we don't always realize that we're weak, or don't realize it as deeply as we should. Weak in the sense that though we can usually muster up some resistance, we lack sufficient strength to defeat temptation every time. Weak in the sense that we lack the strength to rise up to the fullness of being the Christian witnesses God has called us to be, the kind and loving husbands God wants us to be to our wives, the nurturing fathers God wants us to be.

Only when we fully embrace our weakness do we become strong. We especially need to admit our inadequacy in fulfilling the worldly definitions of male identity—be it physical prowess, prestige, or income. That strength comes from the indwelling life of Jesus Christ, who endured our temptations and serves as a high priest, mediating between a holy God and an unholy people.

One surprising way that we see strength manifested is through inner peace. No longer do we strive endlessly, trying to perfect a basically flawed human system, trying to piece together a quilt of accomplishments and legalistic holiness that forms our identity. Instead, we sink our formative roots into the forgiveness and power that come from Christ. Therein lies the cornerstone of male identity.

With an identity secure in Christ, we are prepared to follow the advice of James 4:7: "Resist the devil, and he will flee from you." We don't have to settle for a stalemate with our arch-enemy, barely able to keep him at bay, just outside the range of our weapons. Rather, we can apply forceful resistance to send him to plunder elsewhere. Jesus employed exactly this strategy when he crossed swords with Satan after his fast, as we'll read next.

TEN

Let's Make a Deal

M Y FAMILY'S FIRST HOUSE was located in a working-class neighborhood of Memphis, Tennessee. Our two-bedroom home was so small that having two people in the kitchen practically violated the fire code. It also had a kind of cozy warmth due to the clothes washer and dryer outlets being located in the dining room.

When we decided to move, I verbally accepted an offer to buy our house. A day or two later, a man showed up at the door, glanced around, and beat the existing offer by five hundred dollars. This little incentive was more than two weeks' pay for me at the time. And since I hadn't signed a sales contract for the first offer, I could have legally accepted the second offer, or perhaps tried to play the buyers against each other for the highest bid.

I prayed about the matter and talked it over with my wife. God clarified the situation as a test over what I valued most: my integrity (also known as my word) or five hundred dollars. I could have rationalized the extra money as a shrewd business move. But I knew that God had spoken clearly enough through my conscience, confirming that my verbal acceptance of the contract needed to be kept. I say this not to brag, for it was not without a selfish component: I wanted to avoid any nagging feelings of guilt that would accompany a choice to sell out.

Most men possess a keen sense of deal-making. I actually

weighed the worth of five hundred dollars. What would it buy? Would it amount to much spread out over the span of my life? How much is integrity worth when it's practiced with someone you'll never see again? In other words, I was thinking like a man. We want to know what we'll get when we give something. Even in charitable giving, we have our hush list of expected returns, however selfish or wrong-headed they may be: tax deductions, brownie points in heaven, brownie points with the recipient, and that inner buzz of feeling like a Truly Generous Guy.

What does this love of the deal, this radar always scanning for even the slimmest margin of profit in a transaction, have to do with us and spiritual warfare? Generally, it tends to handicap us. Directing the lion's share of our time and attention to the appraisal of material deals can render us unable to scrutinize the stakes in spiritual encounters.

Satan approached Jesus immediately after his forty-day fast, while he was isolated in the desert—no doubt hoping that physical weakness would make the Son of God more willing to do business with the Prince of Darkness. Jesus proceeded to face temptations which are common to all men and rebutted them with universal truths. Let's take a closer look.

TAILOR-MADE DEALS

So much of Satan's success in spiritual warfare depends on cocky, independent men who think they have all the answers. That's why Proverbs 3:5 warns us: "Trust in the Lord with all your heart and lean not on your own understanding." Satan never fails to show up with his goody bag of temptations, specially picked to skew a man's better judgment. Perhaps you're tempted to confide in a co-worker how poorly your boss handled a private situation. Satan holds out a sweet reward for you: Being one up on someone who's supposed to know more than you do will make you feel wise. And you know from prior conversations that your co-worker will reciprocate by sharing the latest foul-up *he's* observed the boss committing.

Yes, Satan is always ready to make a deal. Just ask Jesus. Satan concluded each of his three temptations by dangling a very sweet plum before the weakened man. Jesus responded differently to each offer. Yet the one similarity in all three of his rebuffs was his practice of quoting from Scripture. This provides a good lesson in how we should fight Satan, whether he is accusing, deceiving, or destroying.

What did Satan offer Jesus? The first two temptations held an implied offer: bread for a very empty stomach if Jesus would zap the stones into loaves; and in the second, a dramatic proof of power, assuming the Father would send angels to guard Jesus if he jumped from the top of the temple. Then in the final temptation, Satan played his best card. He "took him to a very high mountain and showed him all the kingdoms of the world and their splendor. 'All this I will give you,' he said, 'if you will bow down and worship me'" (Matthew 4:8-9).

Apparently Satan was not blowing smoke; Scripture portrays this as a legitimate temptation. If Satan has the resources to offer something as comprehensive as all the world's kingdoms, however he would have fulfilled his side of the bargain, how much more readily will he deal out simpler pleasures that can easily snag our attention?

I want to examine not so much the temptations themselves, but how Jesus responded. When Satan suggested he turn stones into bread, Jesus answered, "It is written: 'Man does not live on bread alone, but on every word that comes from the mouth of God'" (Matthew 4:4). When Satan urged him to throw himself off a pinnacle of the temple so that the Father would command angels to rescue him, Jesus responded, "It is also written: 'Do not put the Lord your God to the test'" (Matthew 4:7). When Satan offered the world's kingdoms, Jesus said, "Away from me, Satan! For it is written: 'Worship the Lord your God, and serve him only'" (Matthew 4:10).

When we boil down Jesus' responses, we find five nuggets:

two negative and three positive. All of them impact men in a special way:

- Do not depend on bread.
- Do not test God.
- Depend on God's Word.
- Serve God only.
- Worship God.

All drawn from the Book of Deuteronomy, these very basic principles immediately arose to Jesus' lips when he was tested. Satan could offer no deal which could supersede these priorities. We would do well to make these principles part of our battle orders if we want to effectively wage spiritual warfare.

DO NOT DEPEND ON BREAD

We've already examined the male problem with identity— that lingering emptiness that motivates a man to prove his worth, typically through his career. The more independence a man has in his job and the more he earns, the more his worth grows in the eyes of the world.

The typical self-sufficient male has got it all under control. Steady paycheck. Insurance for everything. He may even show up at church every Sunday, thereby supposedly paying the premium for salvation insurance with his presence and a token donation. What a guy! You can count on him. He counts on himself, too, and what he can provide. He's a breadwinner.

Unfortunately, God is not counting how many loaves we've won or how fat our families have grown by stuffing the loaves of prosperity down their throats.

"Man does not live on bread alone," Jesus told Satan. Coming off his forty-day fast, an emaciated Jesus wasn't denying that bread would help to remedy his physical hunger. I'm sure he could have ravenously eaten a whole loaf. He was simply acknowledging that bread—symbolizing material provisions—isn't the cure-all for what ails a man. His spiritual hunger holds eternal consequences. Only one thing can fill that void: "every word that comes from the mouth of God."

The spiritual warrior who finds himself depending on material weapons or fleshly strengths has allowed deception to creep in. He will be handicapped in combat as long as he fails to draw upon his spiritual resources. In refusing the offer of bread, Jesus indirectly revealed his own strategy against Satan. He said that man needs spiritual nourishment—"every word that comes from the mouth of God"—even more than physical nourishment.

DO NOT TEST GOD

As a zealous young Christian, a friend of mine deliberately broke his eyeglasses out of a conviction that God would heal his poor eyesight. In short, he tested God. As you might expect, God didn't respond. It's not that God is unable to heal, but rather that his response to our needs remains under his control, not our manipulation.

Satan dared Jesus to put his Father to a test. Jesus could surely throw himself down from a high place and the angels would become his parachute, just as the psalmist promised (Psalm 91:11-12). (The devil is fond of using Scripture to his advantage.) Jesus would not be sucked into Satan's foolishness. Instead, he cited the higher principle, that God is not to be tested.

While God does test his people, he doesn't expect the tables to be turned. God doesn't need testing; he is complete and unchanging. His people are not. God the Father tests us not to see what we *know*, but to determine what we *are* and what we're *becoming*. James describes how this process works: "Consider it pure joy, my brothers, whenever you face trials of many kinds, because you know that the testing of your faith develops perseverance. Perseverance must finish its work so that you may be mature and complete, not lacking anything" (James 1:2-4).

In other words, trials can be the beginnings of something great—provided we give them room to run their course. They create an opportunity to practice perseverance. Becoming more skilled at persevering helps us to complete the maturation process. James 1:2-4 does not say that the mature Christian is one so full of faith that he can snuff out every trial as if it were a candle on a birthday cake. It says that maturity is marked by a fullness, a completion of character whereby someone can count a test from God as a joyful thing. He reaches this point by proving that he will turn to God in each trial and persevere as long as necessary. Every succeeding trial ingrains that response even deeper.

What is the typical male response to testing? Goal-oriented, production-driven men push to get on with business, to resolve any roadblocks. Smash those glasses and see if God will be a team player on this new eyesight-by-faith project. Forcing the confrontation—which usually amounts to testing God—can sometimes be easier than embracing the trial as one that requires you to jump in and fight.

DEPEND ON GOD'S WORD

How do you resist temptation? When you're ready to explode with anger over the expensive tool your child has left outside to rust, you can grit your teeth and count to ten. See a provocatively dressed woman on the street? Turn your head and look the other way. If a subtle opportunity to cut a questionable corner on a business deal starts to look attractive, you can back away by rationalizing that you would probably get caught.

The male in the driver's seat of his life looks for the most obvious way to steer clear of road hazards. How did Jesus resist? He did not rely on willpower, or a well-honed ability to debate theology with the enemy, or some invisible spiritual force-field that automatically repelled every temptation. Jesus employed a simple strategy, evident in each of his responses: he quoted Scripture. Three short words were part of each reply: *"It is written."*

God's Word remains the most surefire weapon to repel Satan's condemnation, those gobs of black tar he loves to spread on so thick. In the previous chapter, I detailed a futile series of defenses a man might employ when Satan condemns him. Let's revisit that same exchange from an offensive position to see how utilizing God's written Word could make a difference. (Scripture references are included, though verses are loosely paraphrased).

Satan: "You missed your prayer time this morning."

You: "So what? I had a late night and an early morning. (It is written:) God desires an obedient heart more than ritual (1 Samuel 15:22). By the authority of Jesus Christ, I forbid condemning thoughts to bother me."

Satan: "You know, that's not the first time you missed a morning prayer time. In fact, you ought to be ashamed to call yourself a Christian."

You: "(It is written:) There is no condemnation for me if I am in Christ. I will not be weighed down by legalistic garbage or my weaknesses because the spirit of God has set me free from the slavery to sin" (Romans 8:1).

Satan: "Well, how about the guys in your men's group? They're expecting you to flex a little mental muscle, as well as some of that spiritual savvy you're known for. And you'll never get all those Bible verses memorized in time. You know you're not going to appear very spiritual...."

You: "My self-worth has nothing to do with how I appear to other people. (It is written:) I am complete in Christ! (Colossians 1:28). In the name of Jesus, get out of here, Satan!" (James 4:7).

You don't have to drop your job, enroll in seminary, and cram your long-term memory full of Bible verses to be prepared for this sort of rebuttal. Of course, spending regular time reading the Bible, studying it, meditating on certain passages, and memorizing bits and pieces are all helpful. The essential strategy in spiritual warfare, however, is to recognize Satan's hallmarks—the condemnation, the half-truths, the worldly and fleshly emphasis—and to meet them head-on.

If you use the typical male approach of trying to justify your failures before Satan, you lose. That's a dead argument. Instead, speak from the perspective of who you are in Christ: flawed, but forgiven. You've signed up for a military career on the winning side. You are complete—full, even perfected—not in the sense of being sinless, but in having the growing seed of a perfect life inside you replacing the decaying husk that surrounds it. Familiarize yourself with the eternal words of truth that confirm these facts, and use them to rebuff the enemy when the battle rages.

SERVE GOD ONLY

During wartime, a soldier is never confused about which side he's fighting on. He wears an official uniform of his nation. He salutes someone, who salutes someone else, right on up to the head of state. And he clearly knows who the enemy is—the ones doing their best to give him an early retirement.

In response to Satan, Jesus proclaimed that we should serve God only. Sounds simple enough, doesn't it? Unfortunately, the choices for men are not so clear-cut. The apostle Paul warned about the multi-faceted attractions facing God's army: "No one serving as a soldier gets involved in civilian affairs—he wants to please his commanding officer" (2 Timothy 2:4). Throughout every age, an abundance of "civilian affairs" is able to lure the soldier in Christ's army away from single-minded duty. These affairs mostly fall into two categories: work and play.

A lot of men—at least those who enjoy their jobs—like to work a lot, whether for the love of extra money or just to thump their chests. Even many a good Christian husband who is not a workaholic has resorted to work as a sanitized excuse for not doing the things he knows he ought to be doing—such as squinting into the sun for ninety minutes while his son sits on the bench through his three hundredth baseball game of the season, or going shopping with his wife to help pick out a carpet that she will ultimately choose regardless of his opinion. Can these mundane activities be more important than getting in a little extra work time? To the extent that they fall within a husband's or father's responsibility to nurture his family, yes.

When not at work, men tend to be at play. We have already mentioned serious addictions—the immorality, drugs, and alcohol that some men abuse in a desperate attempt to prove self-worth or to escape their responsibilities because of low self-worth. A virtually unlimited range of diversions can catch men's attention when they're off the job, such as television, food, excessive sleep, sports, and countless hobbies.

Of course, recreation is a basic need for every man and woman. The key here is maintaining a balanced life, which can be assessed by a brutally honest self-evaluation of one's true god or gods. In the heat of a spiritual duel with Satan, Jesus said that man is to serve God only. He knew that man's choice is not simply serving God or staying completely free, which is how we self-sufficient men tend to frame the dilemma of life and religion. Rather, the true choice is *who*, or *what*, man will serve. Paul made this point in Romans 6:15-23. Everyone is a slave—either the one who obeys the sin nature, thereby submitting to a process leading to death, or the one who obeys righteous principles, submitting to a process resulting in true life.

The command is not just to serve God, but to serve him *only*. We are called to serve God with such a fullness that any other service—to an employer, to a pet personal project, to a church—pales by comparison. In fact, we are called to serve God in all that we do, whether at home, at work, at school, or at play. Being obedient to God's call affects not only what we do outside of church activities, but also the way we approach worship—the fifth nugget in Jesus' rebuttal, which we will examine in the next chapter.

PRIDE GOES BEFORE THE FALL

We can see these principles illustrated in the life of Nebuchadnezzar II, the great king who ruled Babylon during the time of Israel's captivity. The king's military conquests were rarely mentioned in his own records. Instead, he seemed to be preoccupied with his building projects. Nebuchadnezzar is credited with the Hanging Gardens of Babylon, one of the Seven Wonders of the Ancient World.

For all the splendors of his kingdom, Nebuchadnezzar witnessed something even greater through his Jewish captives. Daniel's three comrades—Shadrach, Meshach, and Abednego —refused to worship the ninety-foot tall, gold-plated statue which the king had commanded everyone to worship, so he had them thrown into a blazing furnace. When the three Hebrews survived without so much as a singed hair, the king granted them their freedom and rejoiced in the true God who had spared their lives.

Nebuchadnezzar then had a troublesome dream which Daniel was able to interpret. He said that though the king's reign was extensive, he would be humbled so low that people would drive him away to live with the wild animals. Yet the warning came with an escape clause: "Renounce your sins by doing what is right, and your wickedness by being kind to the oppressed. It may be that then your prosperity will continue" (Daniel 4:27).

A year later, Daniel saw no indication that the king had repented. In fact, he seemed to be violating the five principles we saw in the encounter between Jesus and Satan: do not depend on bread (or any material things); do not test God;

depend on God's word; serve God only; and worship God.

Nebuchadnezzar essentially put God to the test by ignoring his word through Daniel. He also rejected the service and worship of the God of Daniel, who had revealed himself as the only true God. Instead he continued to depend on the material extravagance with which he had surrounded himself. To top it all off, the king had the audacity to brag aloud while strolling on the palace roof: "'Is not this the great Babylon I have built as the royal residence, by my mighty power and for the glory of my majesty?'"

Nebuchadnezzar's boast seemed to add the final drops to the cup of God's wrath. A voice from heaven informed the proud king that he was stripped of his royal authority. He would live with wild animals, eating grass, just as Daniel had prophesied in interpreting the dream.

Very few possess the degree of power and wealth that were at Nebuchadnezzar's fingertips, but humans require no great quantity to fall into the same delusions of pride and self-sufficiency. Each of us has a propensity to depend upon that which is useless, grasping after fleeting goods and turning away from Christ, the only stability in a transient world. And how many times have we been warned that we were displeasing God— maybe not with a booming voice out of the sky, but in a sober rebuke from a friend or a painfully clear stirring of our conscience by the Holy Spirit?

Only when Nebuchadnezzar humbled himself and raised his "eyes toward heaven" was his sanity restored. The once-mighty king responded with worship: "Then I praised the Most High; I honored and glorified him who lives forever" (Daniel 4:34). Nebuchadnezzar paid a high price for his stubborn self-sufficiency, and only his own recognition of his low position brought an end to his enforced humiliation. As we'll see next, humility goes hand in hand with worship, a powerful weapon in spiritual warfare.

ELEVEN

Exalt or Default?

"**N**OW IF YOU'LL TURN IN your hymn books to...."
The words function as reliably as a light switch. Your mind has been engaged with the church service thus far. The men's fellowship luncheon was announced for Saturday, along with the local varsity football coach as a guest speaker. You mentally checked your schedule and decided yes, it would be profitable to hear him speak and to spend some time with the fellows.

Then comes that familiar phrase, "turn in your hymn books." Years of Sunday morning conditioning kick in with Pavlovian predictability. Eye-hand coordination goes on auto-pilot, scanning numbers on the hymnal page corners. Legs lift the torso. Eyes glaze. Brain pushes the remote control button and song comes out of your mouth. Meanwhile, your mind suddenly switches from the Church Channel to the Personal Comfort Channel: *Let's see, I can be out of here by 12:18, pick up some Mexican fast food and eat in the car, get home in time for a quick snooze before the football game, and still have time for some basketball with the guys down at the Y....*

Jesus faced a different sort of challenge in worship. After Jesus emerged from his forty-day fast in the desert, Satan fired one last volley, offering him "all the kingdoms of the world and their splendor" (Matthew 4:9). The terms were simple: Worship Satan.

Jesus rejected that option. Most Christian men, too, have enough sense to steer clear of overt satanic worship. But what is the ideal alternative? Jesus did not respond: "It is written, 'Attend a worship service and holiness will mysteriously drench your soul.'" Instead, he said, "Worship the Lord your God, and serve him only." This is a modified version of Deuteronomy 6:13, in which God's people are commanded to "reverence" or "fear the Lord your God."

Fear, reverence, worship, serve. The Bible uses these words as verbs, which denote *action*. Spiritual warfare embodies activity. After all, military battles are not won by spectators. They're won by soldiers who wield tangible weapons. Of the handful of weapons in the Christian's spiritual arsenal, worship is one of the most easily overlooked. It's not that we don't do it, but that we don't do it with a full heart. We usually fail to give worship the credit it's due because it seems dull and powerless. What sort of damage could we be doing to the enemy by paying more attention to this underutilized weapon?

THE MALE HANDICAP

In an oft-repeated joke, the wife of an aging farmer chastises him, "Why don't you ever say you love me?"

"When we got married, I told you I loved you," the farmer replies. "If I ever change my mind, I'll let you know."

There you have the stereotypical male: non-verbal, non-emotive. Marriage counselors will tell you that women are normally the ones first willing to seek help. It almost seems incongruous to imagine a man moaning before a marriage counselor, "My wife never talks to me. She never says whether I mean anything to her. I don't think she even cares if I exist."

Yet Scripture commands these same male creatures to tell God how much they love him. And not just once, at the "wedding day" of salvation, not just weekly as part of the drone team at church, but over and over and over again. And not just in a religious setting, but at home, in the car, at work, any-where. And not just with our mouths, but with our hearts.

During my college years, I was spiritually languishing, going through a time of falling away that so often occurs between childhood religion and sincere adult commitment to the faith. Then I attended my first Christian home meeting. People (even men!) were raising their hands and randomly saying things like "Praise you, Jesus" and "Bless you, Lord."

Strange. Very strange, I thought. I couldn't imagine joining the cheerleading squad for this sort of pep rally. It wasn't that I would stick out like a sore thumb. To worship as these people were doing would be precisely the way to fit in. Even if I embraced the faith shared by these folks, the price tag of self-abandonment was too steep for this cool guy.

Why does worship, even in its less expressive forms, tend to make men stumble? Because the core of worship conflicts with the core of man. True worship wars against not just males but all humankind. Every Christian has been given a new life, a renewed spirit that desires communion with God. But there's a slight problem: "For the sinful nature desires what is contrary to the Spirit, and the Spirit what is contrary to the sinful nature. They are in conflict with each other, so that you do not do what you want" (Galatians 5:17). That fleshly side of a believer has more interesting things to do than to try to focus on an unseen God, to sing songs to him, to read his revealed Word, to give him the glory due his name.

Complicating that fleshly tendency is King Male who hogs the throne: *If I'm not self-made yet, I'm on my way. I've earned everything I've got, so I don't need to thank anyone for handouts, including God. God helps those who help themselves, right? In fact, God ought to be glad to have me on his side. I'm a deacon and I serve on three church committees. I give his church and his missionaries lots of the money that I slaved to earn. And he's lucky to have me as a well-scrubbed representative to all those hedonists at my office.*

I may be exaggerating a bit, but any trace of that attitude

sabotages worship because the essence of worship focuses on God's holiness. That doesn't mean that God lives in a big white palace or that all his windows are made of stained glass, or that his voice resonates like that of a smooth preacher standing behind a glitzy pulpit. Holiness involves separateness. What distinguishes God from the human race is that he is pure and all-powerful, while we are sinful and completely dependent on his grace and mercy—regardless of our résumé, our paycheck, or our brawn. For a man to please God in worship, he must remain mindful of his nature in relation to God. He is small. A lawbreaker. Unworthy.

Thankfully, the story doesn't end there. The up side is that God bridged the gap when his Son died for all the sin that spews so freely from our lowliness. Furthermore, when we accept God's offer of salvation, the seed of all that is holy about God is planted in the soil of our hearts. Cared for properly, this seed will grow into a mighty oak, offering shade to many and reproducing itself. One of the best nutrients for any seedling is worship.

JUST DO IT

That's all well and good, you may think, but you've tried to get into worship and just never seemed able to log onto that system. Your mental computer screen responds with "invalid password." Don't despair; you're perfectly normal. But you do need to come to grips with these two points:

Worship is not an option. Jesus was quite explicit with Satan: "Worship the Lord your God, and serve him only." Psalm 100:1-2 says, "Shout for joy to the Lord, all the earth. Worship the Lord with gladness; come before him with joyful songs." Psalm 99:9 commands, "Exalt the Lord our God and worship at his holy mountain, for the Lord our God is holy." Ephesians 5:19 says, "Speak to one another with psalms, hymns, and spiritual songs." This sort of emphasis on praise and worship permeates the book of Psalms and surfaces elsewhere throughout the Bible.

We are free from the tyranny of feelings. You're not in the mood for worship today? Fine. Take control. Recall Psalm 103:1: "Praise the Lord, O my soul; all my inmost being, praise his holy name." David commands his soul to come down out of the bleachers and run onto the playing field. The soul falls between that pure flesh (the body) and pure transcendence (the spirit). It is the seat of emotion and will. Man can utilize his will and push the soul one way or the other, sometimes with surprising results.

Evangelist Terry Law recalls how a personal tragedy challenged him to take command of his emotions. Having been in full-time ministry for years, he was in London when he received news that his wife had been killed in a car accident. Numb, bitter toward the Lord, and ready to give up his ministry, Law flew home to Tulsa, Oklahoma, for the funeral. Three weeks later, a friend counseled the heartbroken evangelist to get alone, on his knees, and praise God.

Law gave it a try the next morning before daybreak. The words sounded hollow. Satan accused him of hypocrisy for praying to a God who had killed his wife. When Law considered giving up, God impressed upon him the words of Psalm 34:1: "I will bless the Lord at all times: his praise shall continually be in my mouth" (NAS). Law began to confess the words of that verse, but the devil continued to persuade him to give up.

I waited for some kind of emotional release, some kind of inner help from God, but it didn't come. I was acting on sheer willpower alone. I was praising the Lord in obedience to His Word without assistance from my feelings.... Sometime between two and two and a half hours, I felt a pressure building up inside. It was like water building up behind a dam. I kept praising. It felt like the dam would explode.

Then it did. With a mighty rush, I began to cry with hot stinging tears. My shoulders began to heave. It was like a cramp in my stomach had suddenly released. I raised my hands.... Obedience in praise and worship had brought healing to my inner man.[1]

This experience transformed the evangelist's life, as well as his ministry. Terry Law's eyes were opened wide to the power of praise and worship, and a man's ability to discipline himself to keep God's praises continually on his lips. After that turning point God expanded his worship ministry and directed it to many countries.

BOLD FRONT COMING IN

The healing experienced by Law was no guaranteed thing. A spiritual battle raged, threatening the real possibility of complete loss. During Law's struggle to worship, Satan attacked repeatedly with his usual arsenal of doubt and accusation. Had Law been unable to emerge from his despair, who knows what would have happened? Perhaps his ministry would have completely disintegrated.

Worship is a powerful weapon of warfare. In one Old Testament incident, it played the key role in battlefield strategy. This was no typical battle, the kind we associate with the great figures of military history, such as Alexander the Great, Robert E. Lee, and George Patton. These extraordinary men employed cunning, genius, resilience, and leadership to accomplish great things against formidable enemies. They buckled down, dug deep, and did the job.

Second Chronicles 20 describes a very different military victory and an extraordinary kind of bravery. The incident involved King Jehoshaphat, who was under attack by three armies. The worried monarch proclaimed a fast. He prayed a model prayer before the people in the temple courtyard, extolling God's power and Israel's dependence upon him.

Jehoshaphat concluded his prayer, "We do not know what to do, but our eyes are upon you" (20:12).

God must have been pleased with their corporate humility, for he answered the Israelites while they were still assembled. Jahaziel prophesied, "This is what the Lord says to you: 'Do not be afraid or discouraged because of this vast army. For the battle is not yours, but God's.... You will not have to fight this battle'" (20:15-17).

With confidence in God's promise, Jehoshaphat "appointed men to sing to the Lord and to praise him for the splendor of his holiness as they went out at the head of the army, saying: 'Give thanks to the Lord, for his love endures forever.' As they began to sing and praise, the Lord set ambushes against the men of Ammon and Moab and Mount Seir who were invading Judah, and they were defeated" (20:21-22).

Who won this battle? Not the most ferocious soldiers, or the ones with the best armor, or the most expendable troops who were shuttled off to the front lines. It was the Levites skilled in music, those whose duty was to lead worship, whose bodies would be the first targets for the enemy arrows, and whose weapons were nothing more than tambourines. One might have thought they'd sing something with a military motif, but instead they kept their focus completely on the Lord with an attitude of humility: "Give thanks to the Lord, for his love endures forever."

Words of thanksgiving and praise, not macho bluster, proved to be deadly arrowheads against which the enemy was defenseless. Simple words spoken from sincere hearts brought victory. The resulting ambushes led to so much confusion among the enemy forces that they ended up killing each other. The prophet's word came to pass: Israel would not have to fight that particular battle. Victory had been won on the spiritual plane, while God took care of the physical realm.

Jehoshaphat took worship out of the sanctuary and into real life. You can do the same. During your solitary morning commute, you may be weighted down by anxiety over a difficult situation on your job. With a single-minded focus, try singing a song with lyrics that glorify God. As you do so, it can remind you that while the problem may seem overwhelming, God is much bigger than the obstacles.

Suppose a series of financial blows has left you wishing that God would part the Sea of Red Ink just like he did the Red Sea for Moses. In addition to making wise adjustments in your spending, don't neglect to take your case to a higher court. Remember how the Levites emphasized thanksgiving and praise. Thank God for the bounty he *has* provided—perhaps shelter, electricity, running water, food, clothes, and probably much more. Chances are, you're still living like royalty compared to the huddled masses in many impoverished nations.

The world does not owe you a comfortable standard of living. Neither is God indebted to you. Take time to thank him for every single gift. Realize that God is so far above your limited problem. His resources are so great that it would take only a drip from his faucet to satisfy your material thirst. Remembering that you are his and he is yours regardless of the outcome of your problem, praise him. Praise him!

If you're married and in the midst of serious financial difficulty, join with your family in prayer and worship. If they're not fully aware of circumstances, tell them. Don't let Satan convince you that you'll lose status in their eyes—even if you are mostly to blame for the lack of money. Your mistakes do not nullify God's Word, which declares you as the head of your family, just as Christ is to the church. Act on your headship. Talk as a family, letting the fears be exposed to the light of truth. Lead them in song. Let thanksgiving and praise inflict damage in the spiritual realm and bring healing in the physical realm.

ATTRACTING AND REPELLING

A simplistic reading of Jehoshaphat's story could lead to a false conclusion that victory depends on incantations: say the magic words, and poof! Of course, much more is going on behind the scenes than meets the eye when worship penetrates the spiritual arena.

We need to realize that just as God wants to communicate with his people and his angels, Satan wants to communicate with people and his fallen angels. Worship, in a sense, jams enemy communications by extolling the attributes of God—his power, grace, and mercy. Songs of worship, often based on Scripture, agree with what God has revealed about himself.

Because he remains in rebellion toward God, Satan finds this kind of focus repulsive. And while evil is repelled, the good is attracted. The Holy Spirit and angels—our allies in spiritual warfare—are welcomed when people humble themselves enough to offer up pleasing worship.

Worship can also have a beneficial effect for those who do it. When we decide to praise God, our emotions may not rise up to meet the occasion. But sometimes they follow later, as does the mind. Healing can begin to enliven minds almost paralyzed by endless analyses of spiritual things. This mental paralysis is often worst with men, who tend to be more reserved emotionally and overly rational.

Even men in the ministry are not so "spiritual" that they are exempt from normal male inhibitions. At one four-day prayer gathering of sixty pastors, the group entered into a period of intensive worship. Some of those who were more accustomed to dignified and traditional worship settings were profoundly touched. One man said he'd never experienced the presence of Christ with such reality. One spoke of the joy of being able to worship without inhibition.

The worship leader said, "Many who were typically conservative were so drawn into worship they had a liberty they've never known before, whether lifting up their hands, falling on their knees, expressing themselves with tears or laughter." Their experience is echoed in Psalm 133:1: "How good and pleasant it is when brothers live together in unity!" Men hunger for such a reality—not just a shared intimacy together, but a unity based on their common relationship to the Father.

Consider this intriguing Scripture: "But thou art holy, O thou that inhabitest the praises of Israel" (KJV). How does a being inhabit praises? I can't fully explain how this happens, but praise obviously makes God feel very welcome. When his people humble themselves by declaring who he is in relation to who they are, God meets them. And when God starts hobnobbing with his people, things happen.

Centuries before fission and fusion, Moses was exposed to a source of contamination more powerful than uranium. Unaware that his face was shining with the glory of the Lord, he came down from Mount Sinai carrying the tablets with the Ten Commandments. He wanted the Israelites to come and hear the law, but the people were so spooked that they refused to come near him. Finally he put a veil over his face to tone down his holy glow (Exodus 34:29-35).

Worship, in its purest sense, can work in the same way. When we come into the presence of God, a bit of his nature rubs off. We become more like him, and our countenance reflects this change. Paul draws upon the fading glory that shone on Moses face to explain what happens with those who live under the new covenant of Jesus Christ: "And we, who with unveiled faces all reflect the Lord's glory, are being transformed into his likeness with ever-increasing glory" (2 Corinthians 3:18).

A MULTI-FACETED WEAPON

Worship, then, functions as a spiritual weapon on more than one level: releasing God's power in external situations, but with internal results as well; driving out the presence of darkness and ushering in the forces of light; transforming individuals and the church; and helping us overcome temptations to worship the multitude of potential idols that fill modern life.

Far from being a church-dispensed narcotic for Sunday

morning blues, worship is much broader and much more power-ful than any drug. Even though it is a weapon we men are prone to downplay, we do so at our own loss. We can continue to worship by default, going through the motions on Sunday, or we can aggressively exalt the King of Kings at every oppor-tunity, seven days a week, and so be changed into his likeness.

The more seriously we approach worship, the more we understand the authority we have relative to angels and demons, as well as in relationship to other people. We will explore these elements of spiritual warfare in the next chapters.

TWELVE

Where Do You Fit in God's Battalion?

A YOUNG PASTOR RECALLED an elderly instructor who had taught one of his college Bible classes. The first thing the teacher stressed was the lordship of Jesus Christ. The second concerned Christ's enemy.

"Son, when you address the devil, you address him as 'His Majesty, the Devil,' because if you see him in any less light than his true power, he will bloody your nose," the instructor cautioned him.

The admonition at first seems overblown. After all, the Bible doesn't prescribe any etiquette for properly addressing Satan. Can't Christians harass the devil any way they want to, like little boys hurling insults at someone because their big brother stands nearby to protect them?

We do well to remember the teacher's first point—the lordship of Christ. But we commit a serious error if we ignore the second. Underestimating the power and insight of the enemy and his forces makes us reckless, ineffective warriors.

Several young men in New Testament times learned this lesson the hard way. These Jews who had heard about the control Jesus had over demons decided to flex a little spiritual muscle by doing the same thing. "They would say, 'In the name of Jesus, whom Paul preaches, I command you to come out.' Seven sons of Sceva, a Jewish chief priest, were doing this. One day the evil spirit answered them, 'Jesus I know, and I know about Paul, but who are you?' Then the man who had the evil spirit jumped on them and overpowered them all. He gave them such a beating that they ran out of the house naked and bleeding" (Acts 19:13-16).

Paul and Peter had also been using the authority of "the name of Jesus," but they never came away from such encounters looking like the loser of a heavyweight boxing match. These two apostles knew where they fit in the grand scheme of invisible authority and power. Paul and Peter didn't aspire to be anything more than they were, nor did they underestimate what God could do through them. Ever eager to encounter the foe, they didn't want to miss a single battle to which they were called.

To all outward appearances, the apostles were bold and independent evangelists, traveling around much of the known world and causing Jewish or Roman authorities to bristle at most every stop. But at the same time, Peter and Paul were under God's authority and maintained an intimate relationship with their commander in chief. They understood that being completely available for his service held limitless implications.

God wants the same for every man today. With a basic understanding of the good and evil forces at work in the universe, you are better able to see where you fit. Most importantly, you begin to realize what authority you carry as a full-time soldier in God's army. For no matter how limited you feel as a Christian man, the implications of your position in Christ remain limitless.

A RIGGED FIGHT

Have you ever envisioned the match-up between God and Satan as a tug-of-war between nearly equal powers? Back and forth, back and forth, throughout the past and into the future. And then, as in a grand Hollywood production, God unleashes some spectacular surprises to break this stalemate just before the curtain closes on world history.

In a vague sense, this is true. Good and evil co-exist until the final consummation of God's kingdom. But Christians need to guard against the distortion that their enemy is simply a dark version of God. Merely an angel, Satan stands far beneath God in terms of power and authority.

Traditional theological study identifies nine ascending orders of angelic beings: seraphim, cherubim, thrones, dominations or dominions, virtues, powers, principalities, archangels, and angels. It appears that Satan is at or near the top of this pecking order, what we would call an archangel, such as Gabriel or Michael.[1] Satan obviously has greater authority than other rebellious angels and holds a position of leadership over them. Though considerable, his power is far from unlimited. Because of its limits, and because of the authority we have in Christ, tremendous opportunities for victory lie before us.

We need to guard against one other theological distortion in this regard. As we know, Satan will eventually be defeated. But Christians hold differing views as to how the biblical prophecies of end times will be fulfilled. For example, will the world become progressively more evil before Christ returns to establish his kingdom in fullness? Or did Jesus' resurrection initiate an indefinite millennium that will progressively build the kingdom of God on earth?

Whatever your own beliefs, you need to avoid a form of resignation, assuming that it's useless to engage the enemy because his time has not yet come. Remember that God is not bound by our understanding of time. From his perspective, Satan has already been defeated. From our perspective, the devil's complete subjugation simply has not yet been made manifest. Many battles yet remain for us to fight.

ANGELS WE HAVE HEARD ON HIGH

Most churches don't seem to teach a lot about angels, but don't let a shortage of knowledge discourage you from including them in your vision of spiritual warfare. To catch a glimpse

of their scope, picture a huge force of international sales representatives who stay in the field for a huge corporation. If you
have a job back at headquarters, you may never meet a single
one of these sales people. Yet your success depends on them as
much as on the employees you see every day. Even though we
may never be aware of their activity, angelic beings constantly
serve God on our behalf.

Angels are mentioned in the Bible about three hundred
times. They make an early appearance in Genesis 16, when
they are sent to minister to Sarah's outcast maidservant Hagar.
Angels announced Jesus' birth and rolled away the tomb at his
resurrection. And they're among the primary characters in the
Bible's final chapter, Revelation. The Scriptures tell us several
facts about the roles and authority of angels and their relation
to humankind:

- God made man "a little lower" than angels. At the same
  time, God gave man authority over all the creatures of the
  earth (Psalm 8:5-8).
- God sends angels as "ministering spirits" to serve his people
  (Hebrews 1:14).
- Eventually man will judge angels (1 Corinthians 6:3).
- God uses angels for the security and protection of his people,
  individually and collectively (Psalm 34:7).
- God can use angels to carry out his judgments on those who
  oppose his people (Psalm 35:5-6).
- Angels can be messengers from God (Judges 13).
- Angels can carry on conversations with people (Zechariah 1).
- Angels are integrally involved in spiritual warfare (Reve-
  lation).
- Angels can be powerfully destructive. Second Kings 19:35
  tells us that one angel killed 185,000 Assyrian men.
- Angels are usually invisible, but can become visible. Most
  modern reports describe them as being eight or nine feet tall,

"shining bright, youthful, dressed in loosely fitting robes," according to ministers Judith and Francis MacNutt, who have taken informal surveys at their worldwide conferences.[2]

Elisha's servant learned some of these facts about angels through a chilling experience. Because of his annoying way of knowing just what the king was thinking, the prophet had risen to the top of his most wanted list. Elisha and his servant arose one morning to discover the king's army waiting to launch an attack from the surrounding hills.

"Oh, my lord, what shall we do?" cried the panicking servant.

Calm down, his master reassured him. "Those who are with us are more than those who are with them." Then Elisha prayed that God would open the servant's spiritual eyes. When the servant looked again, he "saw the hills full of horses and chariots of fire all around Elisha." These were probably "heavenly hosts," that is, angels who specialize in doing battle. Elisha asked God to have heavenly hosts strike the invading armies with blindness and the angels obliged.

This particular incident highlights the essential way human beings mesh with angelic beings in spiritual warfare. Angels are here to help us, though we don't give them orders. We pray to God, and he issues a command if our request is in accord with his will. Continuing the above analogy of the large corporation, you may have considerable power, but you cannot give orders to the sales force unless they fall under your area of responsibility. But your appropriate request to the person who does hold the authority will prove effective if it meshes with overall company strategy.

PESKY, BUT POTENT

Demons are the problem angels. Bad company corrupts, as they say, and these angels were corrupted by following Satan in his rebellion against God. These fallen angels share in his continual attempt to short-circuit God's eternal purposes. The evil forces taste success in short-term battles that can be quite devastating, but their plate is heavily laden with frustration because they cannot alter the ultimate outcome. On an individual level, demons can rob us of the peace and joy God wants to give those who follow him. Most frighteningly, they can keep us separated from God, putting us on a course for eternal damnation.

Just as Satan is no more than an angel, restricted in his operations and far below God in power and authority, demons are even more limited. The Bible records numerous instances where Jesus cast out demons with immediate success. Their hold on people seemed almost incidental, like a stray dog that only needs to be yelled at to be chased away. Yet the Bible also reveals the seriousness of demons and what foul deeds they can do.

King Saul, for example, was troubled by one or more demons after he had fallen from God's favor. The mad king twice tried using his spear to make a shish-kabob out of young David, and then spent years chasing him and trying to kill him. In New Testament times, the Gadarene demoniac was so violent that people had to avoid passing nearby. When Jesus commanded the demons to begone, they entered a herd of pigs and drove them over a cliff to drown in the lake below. Until Jesus delivered a young boy at the request of his father, a demon had afflicted him for years by constantly plunging him into water or fire.

One point to know about demons is that you hold a position of authority. If you've been intimidated by movies that attempt to portray the demonic realm, don't let that fear linger. In Mark's version of the Great Commission, Jesus told the disciples to preach the gospel to the whole world; those who believe would be saved. And this is the first sign Jesus gave of those who are saved: "In my name they will drive out demons" (Mark 16:17). The next to last chapter will further explore wrestling with evil forces. For now, remember that God is on your side, eager for you to command evil forces to depart from people or places, using the authority of the name of Jesus.

BEST SEAT IN THE HOUSE

If you look at the whole of God's army as akin to a business, you'll find traits of any large, hierarchical organization. You'll also see aspects of a small group of entrepreneurs, flying by the seat of their pants, mixing responsibilities and assuming whatever authority is necessary to make the next payroll. The modern tendency is to perceive the church as more of the former, while I believe we need to focus more on the latter. Jesus told his disciples that the fields are white or ready for harvest. He's hiring willing recruits, and he's not requiring a seminary degree or a golden tongue for most assignments.

Church hierarchy is evident enough. The Catholic church has the Pope on top, then cardinals, bishops, priests, and lay people, with many specific religious orders for groups of men or women. Each Protestant denomination usually has an overall governing body, regional bodies of authority, elders, deacons, pastors, and lay people. Such order is appropriate and necessary for the smooth functioning of any large organization.

At the same time, the Bible offers a few glimpses of how God's power slices right through these seven-layer church cakes. To begin with, the Father has enthroned Christ in heaven, "far above all rule and authority, power and dominion" (Ephesians 1:21). The King of Kings reigns supreme over every force of darkness, over every ungodly leader that arises on the earth, over every heretical religious or cultural movement. Jesus also reigns over the church, over all its fallible leaders, over all their potentially flawed interpretations of Scripture.

Now comes the part we find more difficult to grasp. As Christians, we are placed with Christ in his position of rulership. "And God raised us up with Christ and seated us with him in the heavenly realms in Christ Jesus" (Ephesians 2:6).

Admit it: This sounds like religious gobbledy-gook. You've probably never had a sense of sharing in the authority of God's only Son. You're still dragging around, living to work and working to live, and you're supposed to believe that you're simultaneously sitting in heaven with Jesus? Let's get real.

So what's going on with this passage?

Seated with Christ. You're not milling around, waiting in the lobby, waiting to see where you'll sit for a meal, wondering whether your reception in the heavenly court will amount to a brief chat while standing. No, you've been ushered in to a place of honor. You're only a janitor at General Motors, but you've been given a seat in the boardroom, right next to the chairman. You only passed out fliers during the political campaign, but you're on a first-name basis with the man in the Oval Office.

In the spiritual realm, you share in the fullness of God's ultimate victory of light over darkness. Because Christ's life dwells inside you, and because you sit with him in the heavenly realms, you can exercise his authority in matters that are in accord with his will. Jesus said, "I have given you authority... to overcome all the power of the enemy" (Luke 10:19).

What about the need for maturity? Doesn't one need to grow in knowledge of spiritual gifting—teaching, evangelism, service, and so on? Yes. But on the day you were saved, you were plugged into God, the main power source. He has delegated to you authority to exercise his power in your daily walk.

In fact, God *depends* on his people to do just that. God could sneeze on the world, forming a hurricane that would selectively drive all the pornography outlets in your city into the ocean, but that's generally not his style. He prefers that the church, as the body of Christ, become more visible as it acts in purity and boldness. God wants his army to climb out of the foxholes and wage war.

Do you ever stand around waiting for the generals (the pastors, the elders, the ministry specialists) to show up at the front line? Perhaps you've prayed about the local convenience store that sells pornography and sensed God wants a petition of protest circulated among Christians. Then go ahead and start it. If you sense something you can define only as an evil presence around the store, pray that God will drive out Satan and his demons from the neighborhood. Operate from your seat in the heavenly places, not from a back-pew mentality.

RELATIONSHIP AND AUTHORITY

Jesus said that we would do *greater* things than he did because he was going to the Father. God is always eager to prove the words of his Son—exaggerated though they seem. We sometimes miss the qualifier, however: "*Anyone who has faith in me* will do what I have been doing. He will do even greater things than these" (John 14:12).

Faith entails relationship. A man of faith does not believe that he will win his co-worker to Christ because of an air-tight philosophical argument, but because he can show that friend a relationship with Jesus that transcends anything the world has to offer. A man of faith will not presume he can tough out his wife's life-threatening illness just because God is good and therefore obligated to heal her on the basis of prayers offered in "faith." Instead, a man's personal relationship with the Father will determine how he uses his God-given authority in praying for healing. And if God chooses not to heal his wife, that same relationship will determine from whom he draws his real strength.

To demonstrate his point, a pastor asked a boy to drive a remote control car down the aisle during a church service. The car made all sorts of turns at different speeds.

"Where is the car's authority?" asked the pastor. The car? The remote control box? The boy? The batteries that powered the car? Authority actually resided in the boy, but that authority was useless apart from relationship. The car had to have a reception device tuned to the proper frequency to respond to the boy's will, as communicated through the remote control box.

No man can respond to his Master's will without being tuned in to God's heart. The seven sons of Sceva were all set to rebuke demons, but they were operating on the wrong frequency. It mattered not that they used the names of Paul or Jesus because they had no true relationship to the real source of power and authority. When they attempted to exert authority they never had, Satan called their bluff. By the same token, we cannot expect much success in spiritual warfare by invoking God's authority when we have fallen slack in our relationship to him.

Developing a relationship takes time, just as responsibility and authority in the work place depend on the practice and maturity gained over a period of months. Part of maturing is learning the heart of God, just as we gradually learn the wishes of a supervisor and the mission of an employer. In the spiritual arena, we learn that God has not given his people a blank check on his authority account. We hold no guarantee of receiving the answer to every prayer. Yet God desires to heal, to save, and to supply all of our needs. As we grow with him, we begin to sense more accurately where he wants to do something special, what's at the top of his agenda, where he's eager to unleash his power against the forces of darkness.

How do we mature with Christ? One way is by learning more fully the various ways our authority in Christ is manifested in daily living.

THIRTEEN

Your Authority in Christ

HERE'S A LITTLE BIBLE TRIVIA: Who was Shammah?
While not much is said about this man, Shammah's claim to fame is worth noting. His name is included among the heroic warriors who served with David: "When the Philistines banded together at a place where there was a field full of lentils, Israel's troops fled from them. But Shammah took his stand in the middle of the field. He defended it and struck the Philistines down, and the Lord brought about a great victory" (2 Samuel 23:11-12).

Ever felt left in the lentils? Outnumbered? Outclassed? Today, you may not find yourself deserted by fellow Christians so much as standing alone, or virtually alone, in a society where those holding a Christian worldview are in a distinct minority. Because you're engaged in a struggle much bigger than yourself, how you handle your own little battles can have far-reaching implications. Shammah boldly defended his field, "and the Lord brought about a great victory."

Each of us has a field or two, or more, to defend. Sometimes we have human help—family, friends, church—but the moment inevitably comes when, solo or not, we are the point men. We are the first to challenge the enemy, to block the first thrust or fire the first shot. Spiritual conflicts are numerous and often bloody. As in Shammah's experience, many warriors have already fled, abandoning the struggle. God is looking for a few good men who know their field and will stand their ground.

DEFENDING YOUR TURF

Rather than trying to examine all the ungodly influences present in our society, let's look at the conflict from the other side: How do you, a Christian man, brace yourself for external conflict? How do you conduct yourself when you're part of it?

Let's try to analyze the full scope of your responsibilities in terms of lines of authority. You may know precisely how the authority flows at work (unless it's a very loosely organized company). If you manage others, you know who they are. And most every working man reports to someone. Even the chief executive of a huge conglomerate remains accountable to a board of directors. A self-employed businessman may be his own boss, but he must please a majority of customers if he expects to keep his phone ringing.

Defining lines of authority and responsibility in the spiritual realm can be more problematic. The rough outline is apparent enough, though not as simple as it sounds in terms of execution. Authority flows from God to the church, and from the church to lay people. Unfortunately, authority and responsibility are transmitted across those two gulfs with about as much clarity as a handwritten note which has traveled across the Atlantic Ocean in a glass bottle.

Because of the inherent difficulties, too many men simply dismiss their God-given authority and responsibilities. You can bet Satan employs his best strategies to convince us to do exactly that. The need to know God personally? Leave it to Sunday services. Topless bar opening in my neighborhood? Let the city council handle it.

The need to be a spiritual head for my wife? Antiquated patriarchalism, no longer applicable to today's self-sufficient woman. Spiritual and behavioral training for my children? The church and schools will provide all they need. New curriculum with questionable values being added to my child's school? That's a problem for the school board and PTA.

Whether you find yourself standing in city hall or walking in the halls of your home, you fit into authority structures in some predetermined way. If you are to be an effective spiritual warrior, you must know what authority God has delegated to you, to what authority you must submit, and in both cases, what that means in terms of your responsibility as a spiritual warrior. Let's consider four areas that pertain to you, whether you are married or single.

YOU ARE A SON OF GOD, SHARING HIS INHERITANCE

"For you did not receive a spirit that makes you a slave again to fear, but you received the Spirit of sonship. And by him we cry, '*Abba*, Father'" (Romans 8:15).

If you've had a kind, loving father, you've had the advantage of seeing a human representation of God the Father. If you haven't, you may have difficulty relating to God as a Father. Whatever the case may be, God has granted us divine sonship. That means we can lay aside any disappointments we may have in our natural father, in our present family, or in any authority figure past or present. We have a Father in heaven who is perfect, one in whom we can stake our identity. Those things any child or adult seeks from a father—such as unconditional acceptance, approval, and love—we have for the asking from God the Father.

Furthermore, we can enjoy an intimate relationship with God. Satan perpetuates a false perception of our relationship. The father of lies holds up a picture of a rich, mean plantation owner who lives a great distance away, and you, the miserable wretch of a slave, laboring all day in the scorching field.

Galatians 4:7 sets the record straight: "So you are no longer a slave, but a son; and since you are a son, God has made you also an heir."

Not just a son, but one with a rightful share of the family inheritance. It's as if you've gone off to college and Dad has given you a new car, blank checks, and a credit card. You're set for action, all because you're a son. Realizing your sonship empowers you to use real authority in spiritual warfare. Ephesians 1:11-19 (NAS) elaborates:

> In him also we have obtained an inheritance, having been predestined according to his purpose who works all things after the counsel of his will... you were sealed in him with the Holy Spirit of promise, who is given as a pledge of our inheritance, with a view to the redemption of God's own possession.... I pray that the eyes of your heart may be enlightened, so that you may know what is the hope of his calling, what are the riches of the glory of his inheritance in the saints, and what is the surpassing greatness of his power toward us who believe.

Open the eyes of your heart! God wants you to avail yourself of his arsenal of spiritual equipment, of the divine power that originates with him. Satan will whisper that you're only a slave, working in futility on the fringe of the master's estate, only sneaking glances at wealth you'll never touch. Confess the truth: You are an heir. You have authority to draw upon every promise of Scripture, to tap into the full power of God. Our heavenly Father desires to draw alongside of us in times of conflict, not to stand at a distance and watch us suffer, shaking his head over how stupid we were to get into such a fix.

YOU ARE A HIGH PRIEST OF GOD

"You are a chosen people, a royal priesthood, a holy nation" (1 Peter 2:9).

Your ability to war against the powers of darkness is not contingent on what the ordained head of your local church thinks or does, or whether you're a deacon or an elder, or whether you've been a Christian for a certain number of years. The Old Testament priesthood has been superseded by Christ; we no longer need a member of the religious elite to intercede before God on our behalf.

The infantryman on the battlefield may report to ten layers of military hierarchy over him and command no one below him. Nonetheless, he's been issued a rifle, a uniform, and a pack full of gear. His bullet will fell an enemy soldier just as effectively as a bullet fired by a four-star general.

On the spiritual battlefield, Satan will tell you you're stuck in basic training, that maybe if you're a good boy for a few years, *maybe* you can do something of minor worth for the kingdom of God. Until then, leave it to the professionals, those with a proven ministry.

The truth is quite different. Robert found himself personally challenged when he attended a seminar for worship leaders from all over the country. He and his wife kept noticing a woman whose strange, annoying, childish voice stood out during the singing, even though she was hitting the right notes. "A lot of people were looking back at her," Robert said, "It got so bad we had to get up and move."

When this woman and her husband came up to the stage to receive prayer, as other participants did at the conference's conclusion, Robert observed her behavior more closely. He sensed that she needed to be delivered from demonic forces—a ministry Robert had practiced only sporadically. Yet no one on the designated prayer team addressed what to him was an obvious spiritual need.

"I thought, 'It's a shame somebody's not praying for her,'" he recalled. "Then the Holy Spirit said, 'You go do it.'"

Though he hadn't met the woman's husband, Robert approached him as the conference broke up and told him his concerns. The man agreed that prayer would be good. But when his wife showed up, he put the burden on Robert to explain the problem and handle the prayer for deliverance, which took more than two hours.

Robert discovered that this woman had been raised in a Christian home. However, her perfectionist parents, including a father in the military, instilled in her a strong problem with self-esteem. That opened the door for a demon to gain a stronghold—one that proved the most difficult to break. Once it was broken, the rest of the deliverance went quickly.

We will explore deliverance more fully in a later chapter. The point I want to make here is that you cannot count on sloughing off spiritual warfare onto someone else. Robert was strongly tempted to stay on the sidelines, writing off the woman's problem as one to be handled by her and her husband, or by the official prayer team, or by someone with a proven ministry in deliverance. By stepping out, he risked rejection, humiliation, and failure.

Many of us remain spectators in spiritual warfare, watching it from a distance the way millions of Americans watched the Gulf War on television. Personal engagement always carries risks, a number of which may not be apparent. Satan will forever tell us to keep away from the front lines because other parts of the body of Christ are better prepared or more worthy for the battle than we are.

Scripture addresses this issue of weakness among God's people: "On the contrary, those parts of the body that seem to be weaker are indispensable, and the parts that we think are less honorable we treat with special honor" (1 Corinthians 12:22-23). God has called the entire body of Christ, from the scalp right down to the toenails, to fight his battles. God's perception of readiness does not always mesh with man's.

Spiritual maturity, of course, has its place in the church. I wouldn't expect a week-old convert to be teaching a Bible class or leading a home group. But most pastors wish they had the problem of restraining church members from taking too much responsibility or authority. More commonly, men fail to walk in the fullness of their authority as members of a "royal priest-hood."

YOU ARE A WORKER, IN SUBMISSION TO A MASTER

"Slaves, obey your earthly masters with respect and fear, and with sincerity of heart, just as you would obey Christ. Obey them not only to win their favor when their eye is on you, but like slaves of Christ, doing the will of God from your heart.... And masters, treat your slaves in the same way. Do not threaten them" (Ephesians 6:5-9).

Clear enough? Painfully so: "just as you would obey Christ." Easy? Not at all. As employees, we may obey the letter of our job description, but our attitude often betrays service not done as unto the Lord. Even those of us who like our jobs find no shortage of grist for gripes. Go to lunch with folks from work and what do you talk about? Stupid company policies, foolish management decisions, irritating assignments. It's almost a national pastime, exempt from scriptural dictates, like driving five or ten miles over the speed limit on the interstate highway because you know you won't get ticketed.

Spiritual warfare on the job flares up when you come against the ways of the flesh and the enticements of your peers in an effort to work as if Jesus himself were sitting in the executive office. But there's an even deeper aspect to your responsibility at work. The Ephesians 6 passage says you should be "doing the will of God *from your heart.*"

Wayne Alderson felt deep within his heart that the will of God was being ignored at his place of employment. Work attitudes became so bad at Pittron, a steel foundry in Glassport, Pennsylvania, that the company had lost six million dollars in three years. With relations between labor and management becoming increasingly hostile, an eighty-four-day strike resulted.

As vice-president of operations, Alderson sensed that the

traditional management by confrontation was doomed from the outset. Both labor and management continued making threats, refusing to budge an inch for fear of showing any sign of weakness. Pittron itself was doomed unless something drastic changed. It was Alderson's vision for change, which he called Operation Turnaround, that ended the strike.

The end of strike, however, hardly marked the end of the plant's problems. It only marked the beginning of an enormous challenge for Alderson. As the son of a coal miner, he completely sympathized with the plight of labor. As a manager, he understood the pressures of running a money-losing industry staffed by hostile laborers. Neither side was the enemy. But because management held the reins of leadership, Alderson knew he had to take the first step of conciliation. And if need be, the second, the third, and any additional steps required to break the hardened mistrust of labor. He knew that the basic dignity of man, sacred in God's eyes, needed to be restored with a continuing dose of Christ-like love.

Alderson wasted no time. He began to walk in the plant alongside the workers, violating an unwritten policy for management. He began to learn the names of the more than three hundred men working in labor. Then he would stop to talk with them, calling them by name. Alderson's white safety helmet symbolized management; he had it painted black, closer to the brown and dark blue worn by line workers. He arranged for the union president to have an office. When a nationwide gasoline shortage hit, he persuaded the president to let workers fill their tanks from the plant's stockpile.

Morale turned around. During the twenty-one months of Operation Turnaround, sales quadrupled, employment tripled, and the bottom line changed from six million dollars in red ink to six million dollars in black ink.[1]

Was Satan at work behind the scenes before Operation Turnaround, scheming to destroy Pittron? I don't know, but the company's diseased condition showed evidence of the same realities Satan likes to foment: mistrust, suspicion, arrogance, failure to communicate, blame-shifting, returning evil for evil. These attitudes and behaviors bring down any relationship, be it between friends, spouses, or church members. They will certainly sink a business.

Whatever position you hold at work, you have the authority to implement a similar plan of conciliation within your sphere of influence. You don't need management approval to treat those below you and above you with respect, dignity, and love. Never underestimate the damage you are doing to the kingdom of darkness by consistently demonstrating God's love on the job.

YOU ARE SUBJECT TO CIVIL GOVERNMENT

"Submit yourselves for the Lord's sake to every authority instituted among men: whether to the king, as the supreme authority, or to governors, who are sent by him to punish those who do wrong and to commend those who do right" (1 Peter 2:13).

This and other passages (notably Romans 13:1-7, Titus 3:1, and 1 Timothy 2:1-2) clearly state that you are required to submit to civil authority as God's appointed administration for the earth. You are called to pay your taxes and pray for the taxman. No pleasant task.

You must also be ready to *disobey* any civil law that clearly opposes God's law. Such situations are rare in many countries, but they do arise. From ancient Rome to modern times, Christians have been martyred for refusing to forsake their faith or pay homage to a false god. Many pro-life advocates have trespassed on abortion clinic property in the name of civil disobedience, suffering jail terms, fines, and occasionally physical abuse during their arrests.

After Peter and John were released from jail, they were ordered to stop preaching about Jesus. "But Peter and John replied, 'Judge for yourselves whether it is right in God's sight to obey you rather than God. For we cannot help speaking about what we have seen and heard'" (Acts 4:19-20). They discerned the higher law and proceeded to obey it, knowing the risks they faced at the hands of men, as well as the reward they could expect from the hands of God.

Within the boundaries of the United States, governmental bodies have promoted abortion, trampled on religious rights, and promulgated amoral grade school curriculums regarding sexuality. What should be your response? Prayer, always. And in your prayer, ask God to lead you concerning personal involvement. No one man can become actively engaged in all the public sector disputes that touch on Judeo-Christian morality, but anyone can join one or two fights, whether on a local or national level.

You would be paranoid to assume that every law or every decision by an elected official that offends your sensibilities must be a manifestation of Satan drawing a line in the dirt for spiritual warfare. At the same time, the legal status quo—from city ordinances up to Supreme Court rulings—reflects the cumulative outcome of struggles with a decidedly spiritual element, like prayer in schools or abortion rights. Satan has won many footholds, some of them having influence all across the nation, especially where public policy comes anywhere close to the misunderstood doctrine of separation between church and state.

One man experienced this quagmire firsthand. His daughter told him that her class never said the Pledge of Allegiance (whose language includes "one nation, under God"). When the father inquired, the principal responded that he didn't think school policy would allow such a profession to be imposed on an entire student body. "We can't put anything on anybody" seemed to be his attitude.

When the father checked with other school districts, he discovered that state law *required* schools to give students an opportunity to say the pledge daily. After further requests were ignored, he finally asked the superintendent's office to issue a dictate that all schools must give students a chance to say the pledge daily. "To my knowledge, every school I'm aware of now does fulfill that legal requirement that they offer students the opportunity to pledge daily," the father reported.

FAITH'S UPS AND DOWNS

This father happened to win his little skirmish. If you survey the scope of Christians taking bold steps at work or in the political arena, you'll find some winners, some losers. It's not uncommon to get wounded in these battles: homes and churches vandalized, jobs lost, lawsuits filed, children ostracized, jail terms meted out. Wayne Alderson, the steel plant vice-president, was temporarily a hero. But when the plant was sold, new management fired him for being too chummy with the workers.

We shouldn't be surprised by any of this. When we act on our faith, confident of who we are in Christ—sons of God, a royal priesthood—we face the occupational hazards of faith champions:

> Others were tortured and refused to be released, so that they might gain a better resurrection. Some faced jeers and flogging, while still others were chained and put in prison. They were stoned; they were sawed in two; they were put to death by the sword. They went about in sheepskins and goatskins, destitute, persecuted and mistreated—the world was not worthy of them. They wandered in deserts and mountains, and in caves and holes in the ground.
>
> **Hebrews 11:35-38**

The same chapter also tells of the high moments of God's warriors. Through faith, they became those who "conquered kingdoms, administered justice, and gained what was promised; who shut the mouths of lions, quenched the fury of the flames, and escaped the edge of the sword; whose weakness was turned to strength; and who became powerful in battle and routed foreign armies. Women received back their dead, raised to life again" (Hebrews 11:33-35).

What's in store for you: quenching the flames or toasting in them? I couldn't begin to tell you. I can assure you of this much: How you respond to the battle is far more important than its outcome. God is looking for loyalty and a firm response, much like Shadrach, Meshach, and Abednego gave when King Nebuchadnezzar threatened them because they wouldn't bow down to the ninety-foot golden image: "If we are thrown into the blazing furnace, the God we serve is able to save us from it... *But even if he does not*, we want you to know, O king, that we will not serve your gods or worship the image of gold you have set up" (Daniel 3:17).

God is in no way obliged to act as a perpetual steamroller, paving the way for us on the bumpy path of life. Yet we are obliged to stay on the path, even when it seems impassable. As we do, the world will gain some recognition, through our commitment, of the one true God.

The Master is always pleased to see you aspiring to be a modern-day Shammah—a brave man and a wise steward, able to give a good account for the measure of authority he's been granted. Regardless of the odds or the size of the battle, have Paul's attitude: "Forgetting what is behind and straining toward what is ahead, I press on toward the goal to win the prize for which God has called me heavenward in Christ Jesus" (Philippians 3:13-14).

In addition to the areas of responsibility and authority, what other issues apply to those of us whom God has placed in marriage? Doing battle on the home front can be the toughest place of all.

FOURTEEN

Fighting on the Home Front

I F ANYTHING CAN COMPETE with David and Goliath as a favorite Bible story for children, it has to be Noah and the ark. These four chapters in Genesis make for good adult reading, too. Yet the author of Hebrews reduces this bizarre tale to a nutshell when he recounts the great heroes of faith. Note what survives in this passing glance: "By faith Noah, being warned by God about things not yet seen, in reverence prepared an ark for the salvation of his household, by which he condemned the world, and became an heir of the righteousness which is according to faith" (Hebrews 11:7, NAS).

By the very act of saving his family, Noah simultaneously defined the disobedient land-lovers as those excluded from divine favor. God played no small part in this drama. First he warned of the flood and detailed the ark's specifications. Then after all the animals and Noah's family were on board, God either literally or figuratively shut the door: "the Lord closed it behind him" (Genesis 7:16, NAS) or "shut him in" (NIV).

God and Noah shut out the rest of civilization ("condemned the world") from the most important voyage in history. It was the ultimate separatist act. If you were inside, you lived; if you were outside, you died. Yet Noah was not guilty beforehand of arrogantly separating himself from his culture.

Even though he was subjected to endless ridicule, he didn't retreat to an isolated place outside of town to build the ark. Rather than remove his godly witness from a morally grotesque situation, Noah went to work right where God found him.

How bad did it get? Genesis 6:5 describes Noah's culture as one where "every inclination of the thoughts of [the human] heart was only evil all the time." Presumably, those in the community had every opportunity to watch this huge vessel slowly rising from the ground, and no doubt they mocked the futility of such a project at an inland site. Noah is described as "a preacher of righteousness" (2 Peter 2:5). If the people had quit jeering long enough to listen, they could have learned what God thought about their wickedness and its coming climactic consequences.

Your circumstances are somewhat akin to Noah's. Though today's church is widespread and the gospel is broadly preached, secularism reigns in our country as the dominant worldview, one hostile to the traditional family and its undergirding Christian values. You are surrounded by adverse social and cultural influences, such as family dissolution, promiscuity among youth, and anti-biblical themes on television.

Yet in the midst of this hostile environment, God has outlined a plan by which you can protect the little sphere of your family. Like Noah's, the ark you must build will hardly be finished overnight. Neither does God ask you to retreat to an underground bunker in northern Idaho to do your task. Rather, he wants you to act without fear in the midst of "a crooked and depraved generation, in which you shine like stars in the universe as you hold out the word of life" (Philippians 2:15-16).

You will also have to struggle with doubt as you hammer day after day after day, seeing little progress and occasional defeat, waiting for the promised rain clouds to form. Satan would have you see all at once the enormity of the task before you, and thereby despair, subcontracting your ark to carpenters and naval architects. "Shouldn't you let the schools and church handle your children's training? This is the twentieth century, after all." "You can't very well hide your family from movies and pop music and the latest trends at school, can you?" "In a time when women pursue their own careers and think for themselves, you don't really expect to have any meaningful influence on your wife, do you?"

Satan's deceptions use endless variations on these themes. Ignore them. At the same time, don't be naïve. The tide of godlessness is rising all around you. Let's see what it means for husbands and fathers to fulfill their calling in spiritual warfare, to follow in the footsteps of Noah, an "heir of the righteousness which is according to faith." "Ark-itects" are in huge demand.

A HUSBAND'S BATTLE ASSIGNMENT

"Now I want you to realize that the head of every man is Christ, and the head of the woman is man, and the head of Christ is God" (1 Corinthians 11:3). Most of the controversy, abuse, and misunderstanding that surround this particular verse stem from its reference to the woman-man relationship. Yet it is only one of the three connections listed. How much less uproar there would be if people focused instead on the two heavenly relationships—especially the headship of Christ.

What kind of example did Christ set? What did he do for you and the church? He obeyed the Father completely. He refused glory. He became comfortable with homelessness and a simple lifestyle. Christ constantly focused on others—healing the sick, casting out demons, and doing other acts of service. He fasted and frequently went off alone to pray. He trained others in godliness. He fed spiritual meat to anyone who would listen.

None of Christ's example is incidental to your marriage. In his discourse on husband-wife relationships, Paul continually interjects the Christ-church parallel. For example, "Husbands, love your wives, just as Christ loved the church and gave himself up for her" (Ephesians 5:25). The husband's burdens, as we examined earlier, mirror what Jesus emphasized in his ministry: loving, purifying, feeding, and nurturing. A man practicing sacrificial oversight will not provoke the difficulties faced by wives of overbearing, selfish, egotistical husbands who pervert biblical "submission."

Every woman has her own special needs, but some are typical of most wives. Satan will do all he can to blind a husband to those needs or to convince his wife to hide them. But as the one assigned a place of headship, the husband must watch over this primary person in his care to see how he can help her maintain a triumphant, well-rounded life. Following are four general areas in which a husband can help care for his wife and deter Satan from establishing a foothold that could undermine their marriage:

Self-esteem. Some surveys suggest this to be women's greatest problem. Many women still remain outside the work force, and many of those who do work hold positions without much influence or personal satisfaction, resulting in a lack of career-related esteem. As every mother knows, children tend to be more of a drain than a fountain. While a mother can draw tremendous satisfaction from her maternal role, the self-centered nature of most children means they will return little to boost her self-esteem.

Guess who that leaves as the esteem-machine? You. It's up to you to remind your wife that whatever mix of duties fill her waking hours, they represent exactly what God wants for her at this stage in life. Or, if obvious adjustments are needed, you need to jump in and help with the decisions and transitions. You need to articulate the needs she is meeting in your children and in you that no one else could begin to address, and tell her (not just once!) how good a job she's doing.

Maintaining a mother's sanity requires a good mix of adult companionship. Even when both partners work at keeping their relationship fresh, sooner or later they discover limita-

from dawn until you put your head down at night, but at least you have a change of scenery, people, and responsibilities. A mother whose life centers around home and children faces the same scenery, people, and duties every waking moment.

Women working outside the home have it tough, too. Studies show that they feel pressured to perform the same nurturing and homemaking tasks they would do if they weren't in the work force. A working woman needs stress relief. Freedom to go where she wants to go is critical—shopping, the library, a museum, a walk, or an out-of-town visit with a relative or friend, whatever.

Men and women with productive and diverse lives generally feel fulfilled. But the Bible warns against busy-ness that crowds out opportunities to be quiet, to wait on the Lord. Do you remember how Jesus corrected Martha? In her frenzy of household preparation for the Lord's visit, she couldn't fathom the proper choice made by her sister, Mary, who simply sat at the Lord's feet and listened (Luke 10:38-42).

Make sure your wife has time for sitting at the Lord's feet, as well as other unstructured activities. Women who are prone to perfectionism present an ongoing challenge in this area. But your wife is worth the effort. If Satan can drag a woman into a Martha-mentality, he doesn't have to worry much about her waging serious war against him.

Spiritual guidance. Many men approach the task of leading their wives in spiritual matters with the same enthusiasm and confidence they would bring to leading a quilting bee for elderly ladies. You may think, *heck, why does she need my help? She's more excited about church and prayer meetings than I am. She prays more than I do. She reads her Bible more than I do. Let's leave well enough alone.*

Of course, not all marriages are like that. In some, both spouses are equally committed, in word and in deed, to seeking God. In others, the husband exceeds his wife in zeal for Christian growth. Whatever your situation may be, one thing is constant: God's ordained line of authority designates you as your wife's head. And since the thoughts and decisions that propel the human body emanate from the head, that gives you a lot of responsibility.

Ephesians 5:26 compares a husband's love for his wife with Christ's love for the church. The passage speaks of "cleansing her by the washing with water through the word." Your wife uses soap to wash dishes and clothes, but you need to be using God's Word to wash your wife. That doesn't mean you have to open an in-house seminary, with you as the faculty and your wife as the only student. But as you read the Bible, ask God to highlight a verse or a principle you can share with your wife. It may be something that you feel applies more to you, which in turn might help her. Or it may be a clear word to help, or correct, or encourage your wife. If God sovereignly placed you in a headship role, you can bet that he wants to use you in it. Tell him you're available. Ask his help.

"Washing with the word" carries a broader application than just teaching and admonishing. Every aspect of how you relate —conversation, behavior, shared concerns, sacrifice—needs to grow out of a life formed by Scripture. If God's "word is near; it is in your mouth and in your heart" (Romans 10:8), and your behavior is progressively remolded according to that Word, you won't be able to keep the suds out of the way. Your interaction with the person closest to you will be covered with God's cleansing Word bubbling up from your inner being. The washing will take place, to an extent, on its own. Satan, author of filth that he is, will be frustrated.

AVOID THE HANDICAP

We have yet to examine one major New Testament passage relating to husband-wife relationships. First Peter 3:1-7 focuses more on a wife's role in submission to her husband, but it concludes with an important admonition to husbands: "Husbands, in the same way be considerate as you live with your wives, and treat them with respect as the weaker partner and as heirs with you of the gracious gift of life, so that nothing will hinder your prayers."

In other words, your spiritual headship does not come with license to be arrogant or neglectful of your wife. Consideration and respect are mandatory on your part. Ignoring that injunction brings with it a penalty. Your prayers—including your fellowship with God and the fruits of it—will be hindered.

Two are made one in marriage. If you fail to show consideration and respect to your other half, you necessarily suffer a lack of wholeness or unity. The head-to-body functioning will be sub-par. God wants those problems taken care of before you move on to other areas, such as dealing with your children.

TRAINING CAMP

"An elder must be... a man whose children believe and are not open to the charge of being wild and disobedient" (Titus 1:6). You may have no aspiration of becoming a church elder, but you wouldn't have read this far unless you want to mold your life in ways that please God. And the test for choosing a good church leader is to see how a man handles authority at home. Children are the proof in the pudding.

Titus 1:6 speaks of two general areas where a father carries authority over his children: instilling Christian belief and training in behavior. Do we experience any spiritual warfare here? You bet. Obviously, Satan attacks any effort to inculcate Christian convictions, and unruly behavior is brother to all kinds of sin.

Being submitted to God helps, but guarantees nothing in terms of how your children turn out. Eli, for example, was a priest at Shiloh. Yet his sons Hophni and Phinehas unlawfully took for themselves choice sections of meat offered to the Lord, and then had sexual relations with women serving at the Tent of Meeting (1 Samuel 2:12-22). Eli's contemporary,

Samuel, was one of the great men of the Old Testament. Yet "his sons did not walk in his ways. They turned aside after dishonest gain and accepted bribes and perverted justice" (1 Samuel 8:3).

No degree of godliness on your part automatically counteracts the basic human tendency toward ungodliness in your children. You face spiritual warfare on two fronts: your child is born with a sin nature (the flesh); and you must battle outside influences (the world and the devil). Let's look at the sin nature first.

Proverbs 22:15 says, "Folly is bound up in the heart of a child, but the rod of discipline will drive it far from him." You don't need a seminary degree to understand that foolishness is not happenstance, but is truly "bound up" in the heart of a child, like meanness is part and parcel of a pit bulldog. Every human being is born with a sin nature. Compared to adults, children usually have fewer skills and less desire when it comes to covering up their wickedness.

I have to repeatedly tear one or another of my sons away from television to clean up some mess that he should have taken care of earlier. I used to think that the inconvenience of interrupting some activity would serve as a negative reinforcement with some lasting effect. My sons would learn that it's easier to pick up their things before a favorite television show comes on—not the highest of motives, but a starting place. But no. Foolishness blocks out this lesson. Living for the present is a strong drive to overcome.

Even though I use every opportunity to let my children experience the consequences of their mistakes, they still seem almost impervious to the lesson. Then, the seventy-ninth time around, I see a small glimmer of light, a dawning awareness that what they do has an effect, and that maybe, maybe, a change of behavior would be in their best interests.

Repetition is one of the hardest lessons of parenthood. You cannot tell children something just once. (Just think how many times God the Father has to repeat the same messages to get through to you!) You cannot depend on one learning experience. They need repeated doses. It's like an army shelling another army across a vast distance. Only a small percentage of the shells may do any damage, but if artillery has been ordered, you keep on firing.

The above verse from Proverbs offers the solution to loosening that bound-up foolishness in every child so that it can be expelled: discipline. It can take many forms. Discipline can mean applying the "rod" of punishment spoken of in the verse, but equally important is employing regular training. One of your primary responsibilities as a father is to teach your children to follow in your steps because your steps are following Christ's.

The whole process can feel very much like a war. Many parents will tell you they don't always win, no matter how godly their home environment may be. But in this area, like others, remember that God does not call you to be a winner, but to be faithful. He has given you the authority and responsibility to train your children. By his grace, you can choose to be an obedient son.

CULTURAL WAR

Satan will try to convince you that you can't protect your children from the onslaught of immorality and amorality, so you might as well give up. As in most of his deceptions, there is an element of truth mixed with the lies.

You can teach children to control their speech, refraining from obscenities, mocking, and name-calling, but they will inevitably hear such talk among their friends. You can expound a biblical perspective on sexuality, but a street-wise classmate can undo it all in two minutes. You can monitor television programs and videotape rentals at your house like a hawk. You can even cut the umbilical cord of cable television, but a night spent at a new friend's house can go a long way toward filling in the gaps.

I'm not advocating white flags of surrender at every junction. Your household is like an ancient walled city, where you need guards posted on every side. You need to take every reasonable defensive measure you can. This includes monitoring your children's friends, teachers, textbooks, music, television, language, and interests. But as in sports, the military, and business, victory does not come to those with a mindset devoted to defense. You need to take the offensive. Seize the initiative.

The Bible offers a basic plan to get you started:

> Love the Lord your God with all your heart and with all your soul and with all your strength. These commandments that I give you today are to be upon your hearts. Impress them on your children. Talk about them when you sit at home and when you walk along the road, when you lie down and when you get up. Tie them as symbols on your hands and bind them on your foreheads. Write them on the doorframes of your houses and on your gates.
>
> **Deuteronomy 6:5-9**

Either parent has the authority to carry out this injunction. But in the Hebrew culture, Moses spoke these words to the father as the clear head of the household. The Jews especially stressed learning language and reading so that every man could understand the law and teach his children, thus fulfilling the commands in this passage.

Taking the initiative proves essential. A father needs to fill each child with truth. Deception is the one common element of the various items in the cultural garbage heap—whether it's pornography, drugs, or sexual licentiousness. They all point to grand fun, personal fulfillment, or harmless excitements with no negative side effects. Unfortunately, a light snack from the smorgasbord of youthful temptations is not enough for a youth to recognize the long-term carcinogenic effects of such morsels. Again, Satan glamorizes true temporal pleasures while concealing long-term consequences.

Foolish youth needs wisdom. While they often look to their

peers for the answers, the best source is their parents. And the only real fountain of wisdom and truth is God's Word. You need to impress the truth of God's Word on your children. It takes repetition, so do it upon their waking, their going to sleep, any casual time they spend with you.

You won't find any passage in the Bible outlining the role of the pastor or the youth minister. Your church ministers can and should be of help, but *you* are your child's primary pastor and youth minister. You've been given the shepherd's role.

Does that scare you? It should. After all, Satan will agree to let your church have your children for a quarter day a week if he and the world can have them the other six and three-quarters days. You and your wife are the only ones with real power to tip that weekly balance in God's favor. Satan desperately wants your children to be molded by the world. You've got a fight on your hands to lead them along paths of righteousness.

MAKING TIME THAT COUNTS

While spontaneous occasions of sharing with your children can be quite fruitful, most fathers find a scheduled time also helpful. A family devotional can be conducted in many ways, but I have included some general suggestions.

Keep it regular. Meal times and bedtimes are less of a fuss for children because they happen every day at roughly the same time. There seems to be no choice about those times, as far as the kids are concerned. You can make a devotional time carry the same weight.

Include Scripture. You don't have to do a full-fledged teaching. One interesting verse can supply plenty of fodder for discussion.

Include worship. Find some songs the kids know, or can learn and enjoy, and sing them. Not only does worship please God, but putting children, especially boys, on the spot to do something as uncool as singing sweet Christian songs helps them understand that strong adults can be tender, too, especially toward God.

Include prayer. If your children are not used to praying out loud, this is a good way to practice. Children (and adults, too) tend to pray for their personal wish list. Put into practice the Christian virtue of caring more for others. Keep track of the needs of family and friends, of your government and of public issues, and pray for them. Impart a sense of going to war to fight for the needs and issues you believe are dear to God's heart.

Make character building one major goal. If you can strengthen your children's convictions daily over many years, you will end up with a strong foundation. It's character—not an unrealistic "just say no" warning—that will enable them to withstand the winds of temptation.

Make godly behavior the other major goal. Children need to see that Christianity is not just good ethics. It's a belief system manifested in everything from the tone of their voices to the way they handle themselves in class. Most importantly, model everything you expect them to say and do. You might as well skip all your teaching time if you're not at least trying to live the same way.

Keep it simple. Those who produce materials for family devotionals hear one common complaint from parents: they've tried it, it didn't work, and they have little faith in trying it again. If that describes you, don't give up. Start out small. Check out materials through Christian bookstores and family-oriented ministries if you need help.

YOU'RE THE MAN

As in many areas of spirituality, mothers are often the ones to initiate family devotionals. God bless them for it; children can learn just as well from them. But what does a father passively teach his children when he abrogates his God-given authority to train his children in God's ways? That Dad is not really head of his family. That spiritual training is only incidental to life (otherwise Dad, as leader, would be handling it). That God the Father (because of Dad's unspoken reflection in the natural father) is a distant, nebulous spirit, disinterested in his children.

Such messages play right into Satan's hands. As long as spiritual leadership remains askew, he can rest assured that the family's effectiveness as a fighting unit for the kingdom of God has been seriously hampered. Fathers, accept your mantle of responsibility. Your family is not going to grade you for your eloquence as a teacher, preacher, or worship leader. Your wife and children simply need you doing what you can to live out your delegated authority.

As you continue to put one foot in front of the other, you will be better prepared for whatever may come. When the activity of evil spirits touches your home or your associates, you will be able to act in God's authority, with hand-to-hand combat if necessary.

FIFTEEN

Hand-to-Hand Combat

PERHAPS IT WAS THE TONE of her voice that they found so annoying. Day after day, the slave girl followed Paul and Silas, yelling things like, "These men are servants of the Most High God, who are telling you the way to be saved."

True, no doubt. But Paul learned early on that something else about this girl explained why her declarations grated his spirit so. She had what was called a "python spirit," named after the priestess of Apollo at Delphi. The term had been broadened to include any fortune teller in the belief that such persons were inspired by Apollo.

From a Christian perspective, no real power resides in snakes or mythological figures. But because Satan can operate in and through any number of mediums, he can produce some very tangible and bizarre results. Apparently he did so with this slave girl. She was a first-century version of the nine-hundred-number psychic lines advertised on today's cable television, though she was probably a good deal more accurate. In fact, the slave girl's talent for predicting the future made her a money machine for her owners.

Finally Paul had had enough of this mouthpiece for Satan. "He turned around and said to the spirit, 'In the name of Jesus Christ I command you to come out of her!' At that moment the spirit left her" (Acts 16:18).

Simple enough, right? Would that every act of driving out a

demon was so finger-snapping fast. Sometimes it is; other times it requires a prolonged steady assault. Sometimes it's dramatic; other times quiet. But one thing remains true in all cases: like Paul or Jesus, you need to be *prepared* to cast out an evil spirit from a family member, a friend, or a home.

Such readiness may sound like a tall order, but it's not. We may dismiss New Testament stories of deliverance as those of Big Guns in a faraway land many centuries ago. But the biggest miracle worker—Jesus Christ—said that those who came after him would do greater works than he had done because he was going to be with his Father (John 14:12).

Because Jesus completed his earthly ministry, returned to the right hand of the Father, and sent the Holy Spirit, you are empowered to do great, even *greater* things. You need to be cautious, but not intimidated by Satan's power. Equipped with the indwelling strength and authority of Christ, you can not only hold your own, but emerge victorious from spiritual warfare.

DEMONS AND THE FLESH

Demons generally need a human body to carry out the tormenting works of their master, Satan. Under the pressure of prayer for deliverance, they may use a person's voice to speak. For example, in some cases they will produce a masculine voice in a female or a feminine voice in a male. The Bible also speaks of cases where high-ranking demons have authority over geographical territories.

Christians cannot be possessed by demons. When Jesus died on the cross, he effectively defeated Satan and his forces. An evil spirit cannot inhabit the same body where the life of Christ resides. To understand this spiritual principle, consider the fact that healthy people occasionally get sick. This doesn't mean that they will stay sick, or die, or that their physical constitution is fundamentally flawed. In the same way, godly people still stumble and fall into serious sin, perhaps through the influence of a demonic spirit. But they are not thereby given over to Satan and doomed to eternal damnation.

If you belong to Christ, neither Satan nor a demon can negate the new life inside you. Believers are not *possessed* by demons, but rather *oppressed*. As an analogy, imagine an evening fishing trip. A mosquito starts buzzing around your head as the sun sinks below the horizon of the marshy lake. Then several more arrive to check out this juicy morsel of your exposed flesh. Pretty soon you're swatting mosquitoes like crazy, with a few casualties on their team but many more bites scored on you. These buggers never get inside of you, but they sure can make your life miserable.

Demons, too, harass you. Like Satan, they do anything they can to keep you from pleasing God and living at peace with God. Demons have fairly distinct personalities, with appropriate names like self-hate, fear, or lust. These particular characteristics indicate how demons torment a person. People often are afflicted by more than one demon—in fact, dozens in some cases.

The harassment frequently takes the form of excessive, compulsive, or obsessive behavior. A demon of anger may drive a person to lose his temper at every opportunity, to flare up way out of proportion. A person troubled by a demon of anger is likely to say, "I just don't know what comes over me. I know I shouldn't get that angry. I've repented of this and asked God to help me. I feel so rotten after an outburst that I almost hate myself."

In such cases, repentance does not resolve the difficulty. Even though the sinful expression of anger is a carnal act, this sort of uncontrollable behavior isn't rooted in the flesh. The fundamental problem is a demon that must be commanded, through the authority of Jesus Christ, to quit tormenting the person. An adage in deliverance ministry underscores this principle: you cannot cast out the flesh, nor can you repent of a demon. By the same token, you can't crucify a demon, but you can the flesh. You can't cast out the flesh, but you can command a demon to leave.

Distinguishing between the flesh and demonic activity is the most basic area of confusion in deciding whether or not to pray for deliverance. More bewildering cases involve those exhibiting more dramatic symptoms: claiming to hear voices, being compelled repeatedly to commit suicide, manifesting multiple personalities, gushing forth vulgarities, blasphemies, and nonsense, and so on. Any of those symptoms could be demonic in origin or they could be psychological or physiological. In instances of apparently severe mental or emotional disturbances, it's best to consult with medical professionals in addition to those more experienced in discerning the demonic realm.

WHAT TO EXPECT

What if demonology is new to you and no one in your church knows or cares about it? Perhaps you don't know anyone exhibiting the kind of bizarre behavior that would make you suspect demonic harassment. Should you file this topic away as just another Christian curiosity, or should you be hunting for demons as if they were hidden chocolate eggs on Easter morning?

The answer lies somewhere in the middle. We have touched on the plentiful sources of evil in modern American culture. If you have a family, you must look after not only yourself but others as well, including children whose characters are still in the formative stages. They live and breathe in a world which offers a ready array of material and sensual gratification. A child's flesh hungers to sample this tantalizing smorgasbord, while the devil busily employs his expertise as a caterer.

In spite of all that adversity, we can focus on the good in life more than the evil. Fill your household with demonstrations of godly, selfless love. Fill your family's minds with Scripture. As Philippians 4:8 commands, think true, pure, and wholesome thoughts. Devote your energies to searching for God, not demons. As God's presence begins to increase in your home, any demon at work will be forced to become less and less powerful, leave and harass someone else, or manifest itself. If a manifestation occurs—typically a compulsive sin or some strange behavior that cannot be accounted for by ordinary explanations—then prayer for deliverance is in order.

An assistant pastor named Bruce needed prayer for deliverance right under his own roof. One of his young daughters seemed unusually tense and didn't want to eat anything at all. Seeing this as strange behavior, Bruce called his friend, the late Don Basham, who had a deliverance ministry. Basham set the girl on his lap and explained to her that he believed some unholy spirits were tormenting her. Using the authority of Jesus' name, he prayed for the spirits to leave her.

"She just suddenly relaxed," the father recalled. "She was totally free." Since then, Bruce said, he and his wife have practiced that kind of prayer for each other and their children when any problem appears to have an unnatural root.

"I don't make a big deal out of it, saying, 'I think you've got a demon!'" Bruce said. Rather, he said, it's a matter of sticking to the basics: addressing the spirit from the vantage point of the authority of Jesus' name, confirming the freedom that he paid for by dying on the cross, and commanding the spirit to leave.

Other experiences with demons are not so tame. Bill engaged in deliverance ministry for twenty years without ever meeting resistance. Then one day he and some other men were praying for a man who became physically violent. Even though the combined weight of the men holding him down totalled about nine hundred pounds, they couldn't sufficiently restrain him.

"He still came up with his hand for my throat," Bill vividly recalls. But God's power met that of the enemy. "When I put my hand in his, it would just collapse." Whenever Bill addressed the demon in the name of Jesus, commanding it to leave, the man's head would turn away. Then he would lunge again with his hand, trying to choke Bill. After about twenty minutes of prayer, the demon finally gave up and departed.

A WELCOME MAT FOR DEMONS

What's even better than getting rid of a demon is slamming the door in its face before it ever gains a foothold. To do that, you need to know how they come to harass people.

One common way is through addictions, such as smoking, drinking, or stealing—behaviors which can also be a symptom of demonic influence. Sinful behavior indulged in repeatedly may not constitute an addiction, but may still open the door to demonic activity. For example, a person may like to drink to excess one or two times a month, but does not suffer from alcoholism. In either case, the habit can put out a welcome mat for a demon. The tendency to hide most such sins—gluttony or pornography addiction, for example—also gives an advantage to the Prince of Darkness, whose ways thrive under cover. Exposure to the light of truth always throws Satan's forces back.

A more direct route for demonic influence is through the occult, which includes reading horoscopes, dabbling in astrology, fortune telling and witchcraft, or playing with an Ouija board, tarot cards, or the modern game of Dungeons and Dragons. All of these activities direct the participant on a search for supernatural power apart from God. Though Satan or his demons may not be mentioned by name, this kind of invitation falls directly within their realm.

Another way demons can gain access is through a serious accident or other shock, such as the illness or death of a loved one, or through abuse (sexual, physical, or emotional) that causes extreme physical or mental pain. The trauma to the emotional system can open a door for demons, just as certain illnesses can lower the body's defenses against infections.

Heredity provides another common pathway. Strange as it seems to the rational, twentieth-century mind, the prospect of curses or sins being passed from generation to generation appears as fact in the Old Testament (Exodus 20:5; Leviticus 26:39). To use the physical comparison again, it doesn't seem fair when a person is born with a birth defect, but the harsh reality is that some faulty traits get passed from parent to child whether we like it or not.

WRESTLING WITH EVIL FORCES

For these or similar reasons, you may find yourself or some-one close to you in need of prayer for deliverance from demonic influence. As I pointed out earlier, one of the major stumbling blocks is simply figuring out whether you're facing a problem that is demonic in nature or one that is carnal. Has a person been wrestling with a problem as if it were sin—repenting, praying, fasting, reading the Bible, employing self-discipline—but continuing to fail? If so, that's a sign of potential demonic activity.

Demons tend to torment or terrify people, making them feel at the mercy of some other power and instilling abnormal fears and desires. For example, a man may be plagued with unusually strong temptations to shoplift, and so he gives in. Even though he tries repeatedly to break the pattern, he doesn't seem to be able to control himself. The isolation and failure produce deep shame. Whatever the specific problem, the sufferer has a sense of being enslaved to it, compelled to repeat the behavior or thought pattern. The demon usually gains control through some initial weakness in the flesh. So even after successful deliverance, a person needs to use com-mon sense and self-discipline to avoid the circumstances that could reignite the problem.

Many professionals describe addictions as producing the same sort of effects. People can become addicted to sub-stances—such as drugs, alcohol, or food—which can be traced to chemical deficiencies in the brain. Or they may suffer from closet compulsions—such as shopping, work, sex, or worry—which can produce the same kind of drivenness. Full recovery sometimes comes only through working a rigorous program such as the Twelve Steps of Alcoholics Anonymous. If a person does suffer from an addiction, demons could still be at work to add even more torment. While deliverance may not provide the whole answer, it may be worth a try.

Should you pray for deliverance by yourself? You can, especially if a situation seems to need immediate attention and no one else is around. Remember, the authority lies in Christ, not in a pastor or a large gathering of believers. But I highly recommend having one or two other people to pray and counsel with you if at all possible, even if they're not especially experienced in this sort of ministry.

There is strength in numbers, as well as wisdom. Another believer may discern things that you miss, like which direction to pursue in prayer, or what deception the demons are employing. And they will try anything. Speaking through the person being prayed for, they may threaten those praying, they may try to bargain, they may say they're leaving when they're not, and so on.

Whether you're praying for yourself or someone else, here are five steps common to most situations requiring deliverance:[1]

1. The person seeking deliverance should have an attitude of humility. The subject should be completely honest about the problems that culminated in this point of desperation. He or she should confess all sin and particularly resolve any problems with unforgiveness or bitterness toward anyone. Any occult activities should be renounced, even if the demonic manifestation seems to be unrelated to the occult. Be prepared for a more difficult time of prayer if a person has been strongly active in the occult; this seems to be Satan's best opportunity for gaining a powerful stronghold.

As Don Basham used to teach, a person seeking help may have to choose between dignity or deliverance. The deliverance process itself can produce some nasty side effects, as we will see, but this is to be expected when you are dealing with the Prince of Darkness. Don't take it personally.

2. Identify the spirit. You may already have a good idea as to what has been tormenting the person. If not, invite God's presence and the direct leading of the Holy Spirit. Command every demon, by the authority of Jesus, to identify itself. Through the person's mouth, they often do this. The demon may also manifest itself in ways that betray its presence. For instance, a man afflicted with a demon of masturbation may begin to curl or clench his fingers when the prayer begins.

3. Command the spirit to come out. First, ask for God's protection on those praying, as well as on their households. Then using the authority of Jesus, renounce the spirit by name and deny it permission to torment the person. Command it to leave.

A demon will sometimes object, argue and threaten. It's not uncommon for one to say, "I'm going to kill you!" or claim that it's going to inhabit those who are praying. These are typical satanic tactics of fear and deception. Respond verbally from your place of strength: "I'm a son of God and I've asked his protection for us. You have no right to touch us."

4. Expel the demon. The person should breathe out sharply, an action that seems to complete the expulsion of the evil presence. Some people exhibit a more dramatic variation, like coughing, crying, screaming, gagging, or even vomiting.

This is not to say that the subject should do whatever comes to mind. During deliverance, there may be a tendency to act or speak violently. Usually the person retains self-control and has enough will power to simply refrain from objectionable behavior.

The release of one demon may expose others. If the person lacks peace, or if other demons identify themselves, stick with the process.

5. Maintain the deliverance. Those set free from demonic influence should praise God for the gift of liberation. They should guard their thought life and lifestyle. Like a recovering alcoholic, they need to refrain from flirting with the same thing that got them into trouble. They need to seek out Christian fellowship, since the mutual support that comes through associating with fellow comrades in arms provides a good deterrence for Satan. Those who stay alone too much, or who choose to associate with ungodly friends, open themselves up to renewing their former bondage. On the other hand, God is present where his people gather, and "where the Spirit of the Lord is, there is freedom" (2 Corinthians 3:17).

Maintenance has a broader sense as well. One worship leader considers deliverance as a somewhat routine part of the Christian life. He and his wife regularly perform a self-diagnosis for the possible need of deliverance. "I kind of look at it as a five-year maintenance plan," he said. He reasons that the time he spends in praying against demons usually doesn't take long, so that he has little to lose and much to gain.

A CASE STUDY

Although more dramatic than most cases, the following story illustrates many of the points in these five steps. A man had gone back and forth with practicing homosexuality. Eventually he divorced his wife due to problems relating to the homosexual lifestyle, though he wasn't certain if she even knew about his homosexuality. The man had a sincere desire to permanently forsake this behavior, partly because he feared sexually transmitted diseases and also because he hated being manipulated by his homosexual partners.

He finally became so desperate that he sought help for deliverance from a pastor-counselor and another man. After talking with him further, they discovered that this man had some association with satanists. He appeared to be afflicted with demons relating to lust, lying, homosexuality, bestiality, and other gross perversions such as consuming urine and feces. During prayer, the demons responded to their eviction notice by throwing the man into convulsions.

"Some kind of green slime was coming out of his mouth and nose," recalled the pastor. The demons also began speaking to the men who were praying. "One of the most hideous ones I remember was a feminine voice," the pastor said. "This guy became almost totally feminine at one point."

The prayer lasted over an hour as each demon was addressed and commanded to leave. Then the man slumped to the floor. Five or ten minutes later, he became alert and was fine. While this man's deliverance was complete by any objective standards, that didn't mean all spiritual warfare was over. He continued to struggle with the same temptations. When he unwisely visited with some of his former partners, they told him how much they loved him and missed him.

Fortunately, the man began to set his will more firmly on a different course. He began to associate more with Christian friends, one of whom played a key role in the man's ability to overcome the continuing temptations. The friend simply made a phone call and let the embattled man know, "I've been praying for you."

In this case, maintenance was a day-by-day process—certainly nothing to take for granted. "He was working out and walking out his salvation in fear and trembling," said the pastor, referring to the admonition in Philippians 2:12.

PENALTY FOR POOR MAINTENANCE

How easily this man's story could have turned out differently. Jesus provided some keen insight into what happens when a demon leaves a person: "When an evil spirit comes out of a man, it goes through arid places seeking rest and does not find it. Then it says, 'I will return to the house I left.' When it arrives, it finds the house unoccupied, swept clean and put in order. Then it goes and takes with it seven other spirits more wicked than itself, and they go in and live there. And the final condition of that man is worse than the first" (Matthew 12:43-45).

Another pastor recalled a twenty-eight-year-old friend who

had returned to school in Georgia, where the pastor was then in youth ministry. His friend, the son of a minister, tended to be depressed most of the time. Because he had made known his suicidal intentions, church friends tried to stay in close touch. Unfortunately, they only found him gone from his room whenever they came calling. Finally, his friend showed up at the pastor's office.

"He was irate," said the pastor. "He said, 'You wonder where I've been?' He said, 'I've made new friends, and now I realize my problem was that I was demon-possessed. It took all-night prayer before I finally got delivered.'"

So why was he angry? He felt someone at his church should have recognized his need for deliverance and prayed for him accordingly.

"He cussed me out, four-letter words and all," the pastor said. Though the extent of this man's deliverance could not be readily determined, it was clear that if demons had left, it appeared that Jesus' warning of Matthew 12 had come to pass.

"He had been meek and depressed; now he was angry and proud," the pastor said. "He wasn't helped in the long run."

This man's predicament illustrates the importance of the root attitude mentioned earlier: ongoing freedom requires walking with God with a full heart, practicing the positive, affirmative aspects of the normal Christian life. Without this sort of constructive, offensive posture, all the defensive measures in the world to drive out the enemy will not get you very far. The same applies for every person under your care.

OTHER DEMONIC INFLUENCE

So far we have dealt with the effect of demons that attach themselves to individuals. The well-trained spiritual warrior must also be aware of the influence of Satan and his demons over a physical area. It could be as small as a home or as large as a nation. If demonic harassment is not precisely tied to one person, then how should we pray?

All families experience periods of bickering and confusion. Nerves become frazzled and stay raw. But when arguments become the norm, not the exception, a father should step back and discern if there's more at work than simply carnal natures engaging in normal conflicts.

"It's harassment if it's set in the context of real commitment to Christ," observed one minister. Once he and his wife identify what appears to be a concentrated attack in their home, the battle is largely won. They rebuke whatever spirit—such as fatigue or selfishness—has begun to take root.

You may also notice demonic influence in unfamiliar territory. One man took some Boy Scouts on a camping trip, planning to sleep in a cave. As they were about to set up the gear, the man got an uncomfortable, threatening feeling about the cave. He prayed about it and felt the Lord wanted them to camp somewhere else, which they did.

The man later learned that the cave was a favorite hangout for occultists. Though he was not used to discerning those kinds of promptings, the incident provided a concrete experience so that he could be more sensitive in the future.

When you move into a previously occupied residence, it's a good idea to pray in each room for a complete cleansing of any evil remnants. As you pray, the Holy Spirit may reveal a sense that sinful activities had been common to one room, such as drug abuse or sexual perversion. Even if there are no specific revelations, you can use your authority as head of your household not only to commit your physical dwelling to God but to command any lingering evil presences to depart.

DUELING PRINCES

While Satan and his demons can exert a strong influence over a household or a cave, they can also take on a larger area—a neighborhood, a city, or a nation. Several biblical accounts vividly illustrate this possibility. You don't have to try to plot the entire extent of Satan's real estate portfolio, nor do you need to single-handedly take on the burden of toppling his dynasties. You do, however, need to be aware of how Satan's strongholds can be spread over the earth, how you may be confronted with them, and how you can respond.

After surviving the lions' den, Daniel plunged into some heavy-duty spiritual warfare. After he had mourned and spent three weeks on a strict fast (no meat, choice foods, or wine), God granted him a vision. He saw an angel, probably Gabriel, who gave him an intelligence report on the last few weeks of spiritual warfare: "Since the first day that you set your mind to gain understanding and to humble yourself before your God, your words were heard, and I have come in response to them. But the prince of the Persian kingdom resisted me twenty-one days. Then Michael, one of the chief princes, came to help me, because I was detained there with the king of Persia" (Daniel 10:12-13).

"Prince" refers to angels with some higher degree of authority, commonly known as principalities. The Bible does not explain how this conflict between principalities actually plays out. Those used to envisioning hand grenades and surface-to-air missiles may not be able to comprehend the realities of heavenly combat. But the revelation is clear. Daniel initiated something in the court of God. Gabriel was eager to respond, but he met no small amount of resistance—enough to delay the mighty archangel three weeks. Gabriel couldn't handle the hindrance by snapping his fingers or saying "Be gone in the name of Jesus!" Only with the arrival of a reinforcement—Michael, another archangel—could this mighty angelic warrior respond to Daniel.

And that didn't settle things for good. Gabriel went on to say, "Do you know why I have come to you? Soon I will return to fight against the prince of Persia, and when I go, the prince of Greece will come" (Daniel 10:20). Not only was the evil principality over Persia still alive and kicking, but so was a similar power connected with Greece, with whom Gabriel would have to contend.

DISCERNING THE DARKNESS

All this data was passed to Daniel from an angel in spectacular array: "a man dressed in linen, with a belt of the finest gold around his waist. His body was like chrysolite, his face like lightning, his eyes like flaming torches, his arms and legs like the gleam of burnished bronze, and his voice like the sound of a multitude" (Daniel 10:5-6).

Should you expect to see a stunning angelic messenger every time you seek a response from God through prayer and fasting? No, though many Christians throughout the centuries have reported encounters with angels. You may also want to consider the downside of this sort of close encounter of the angelic kind. Daniel recalled, "I had no strength left, my face turned deathly pale and I was helpless" (10:8). The incident was so overwhelming he could barely breathe (10:17). Merely a lad, Daniel was caught in the midst of something almost out of his league. This was spiritual combat for men, not for boys.

Discerning what principalities are struggling over a city to maintain their domains doesn't usually entail this sort of heartstopping drama. A more common experience was reported by a couple who lived on the outskirts of a Canadian city. On their frequent trips into the city, the husband and wife noticed an intangible change whenever they would pass under a particular railroad trestle which posted a welcome sign for the city. They usually felt very sleepy and began to yawn. The couple also noticed they tended to get short with each other.

They eventually learned that the city hosted more than the usual share of Satan worship, witchcraft, and homosexuality. One year the local newspaper printed a running battle of letters from white witches and black witches as to the proper understanding of Halloween.

A man in full-time ministry had a more tangible brush with the enemy during his visits to a city in the Midwest. On one such occasion, he was conducting a seminar on spiritual warfare for four hundred people in a school auditorium. The man was having trouble collecting his thoughts; the crowd was restless.

"I noticed people coming in the back door dressed in black," he said. "They weren't part of the seminar at all. Some of them were muttering, making a disturbance. The seminar had been infiltrated." The uninvited visitors were connected with the occult. By their disruptive presence, they made it known that Satan is not quick to hoist the white flag.

This organized resistance was not an isolated incident in this location—either for those enlisted on God's side of spiritual warfare or for the general population. The speaker learned that this city was a known haven for Satanism—one of many such cities where Satan appears to have gained a sturdy stronghold either through direct occult practices or a heavy concentration of sinful activity.

How do you respond when a demonic stronghold appears to be seriously disrupting a planned activity? In this case, the minister began to pray, asserting the authority of God and rebuking the presence of the enemy. Some of the seminar participants escorted the satanists out. That went peacefully, but the battle was hardly over. The following day, a Sunday, the conference group returned to the school facilities to discover that someone had left a gruesome calling card left by overnight vandals: hamsters and gerbils had been chopped up and their blood splattered on the walls.

In most cases, the spiritual character of a city is not something that will necessarily jump out and identify itself. Physical appearances—the number of churches, general cleanliness, and so on—can deceive. Practiced discernment is one way to judge if a city or country has a spiritual bent one way or the other. In some cities, common sense and observation offer telltale clues. For example, satanic strongholds are to be expected in cities such as Los Angeles, which is the leading city in the United States (if not the world) for the production of pornography and which has major problems with crime, gangs, and drugs.

I encourage you not to jump into renouncing all sorts of satanic strongholds single-handedly. In fact, never take on territorial spirits alone but only in a group of wise and discerning Christians. Make sure that God is directing you to contend with a particular stronghold. If you charge into a battle where God hasn't called you, a backlash from Satan could cause you more trouble than you're prepared for. No large-scale spiritual warfare should be undertaken without consulting God.

Satan is ultimately seeking souls, not soil. Yet he knows that maintaining a strong influence over the places where people eat, sleep, and work, day after day, works to his advantage. As those charged to be alert to the devil's schemes, we have to realize that spiritual warfare sometimes takes on this territorial dimension. If you find yourself walking the point for your patrol in enemy territory, sensing spiritual infiltration before anyone else does, be ready for a spiritual fight.

You may have matured in your Christian walk to the point that you can identify your strongest areas of gifting—perhaps teaching or service. Praying for deliverance may be something you wanted to specialize in as much as you wanted to learn how to repair high-voltage power lines in the midst of a sleet storm. That's okay. Just remember that the war with Satan may have its lulls, but it never really stops, and "no one is discharged in time of war" (Ecclesiastes 8:8). If you are summoned to the front lines, be ready. God always equips his people for the fight to which he calls them.

SIXTEEN

"After You Have Done Everything..."

B EFORE FOLLOWING A WHIM to enlist in the army during wartime, I would carefully weigh several considerations. What am I leaving behind—job, safety, security, comforts, family? Could I be crippled? Disfigured? Captured? Tortured? Killed? What would I gain—adventure, combat awards, career connections, battlefield spoils, souvenirs, a new sense of maturity, the satisfaction of helping my country?

Jesus issued fair warning to his potential recruits. "Count the cost," he said, like a builder estimating a construction project before submitting a bid, or like a king gauging his enemy's strength before jumping into battle. Jesus wasn't simply talking about the moment of salvation, the crossing over from one kingdom to another. He was seeking disciples who would go the distance—build the tower to completion, fight the war until its final victory.

Having examined much of the basics of spiritual warfare, let's step back and look at what's involved with going the distance. Three broad considerations come into play:

The risks: The roar of Satan, the prowling lion, can turn into an empty boast when God's power triumphs. Or it can be the last thing you hear before those vicious jaws clamp down on your head. What is your risk? Can you minimize it?

The cost of participating: How much baggage do you need to shed to make you lean enough to go the distance?

The spoils: God is good and just. He wouldn't call you to wage war with his enemy if there weren't some wonderful rewards—frequently here, but always in heaven. What's in it for you?

THE RISKS

Mike and his family had seen better years. Much better.

In April, their daughter passed out while on a mission trip to Guatemala. Suspecting a petit mal seizure, the doctors performed electro-scans and other tests when they returned home. The exact cause was never determined. The girl also experienced a very difficult year at a new school.

In May, Mike's son was injured in the last baseball game of the year, ruining his chances of playing on a post-season league. Insurance provided only partial coverage for the physical therapy he needed. His son faced his worst year ever in high school.

In June, Mike's wife began suffering from a thyroid problem and had to see several doctors. The illness sapped her energy, contributing to tensions between her and Mike over mounting medical bills. The couple also experienced stress surrounding their decision to leave a church where they had long been members.

"When all these medical bills hit at the same time, we were wondering 'What is going on?'" Mike said. "You start putting two and two together, and that's why I feel Satan was bent on destroying our family."

The breakthrough came when they humbled themselves before God, praying diligently and asking for his priorities in their lives. Such assaults are not uncommon, especially among those engaged in full-time Christian work or a ministry which attacks Satan head-on. Because of their wholesale dedication to fighting his kingdom, such soldiers often report that Satan's response can become particularly intense.

One pastor had a small ministry assisting people who wanted to leave behind occult beliefs and lifestyles, as well as providing counseling for their families. He recalled how one member of his team, a deputy sheriff, experienced a string of disasters over three to five years after his involvement began.

The deputy had a rash of four to five car wrecks on the job. His tires were slit on two occasions. His mother had cancer surgery. His wife suffered repeated asthma attacks and nearly died. His daughter was physically threatened by fellow students. His father was wrongly accused of molestation and lost his teaching position, even though he was later found innocent. After suffering three heart attacks, his father died two months after leaving his job.

Those experiences reflect some of the ways Satan strikes back against God's people. He typically targets the areas of health, peace, faith, reputation, and finances.

Health: Don't interpret Satan's desire to kill you as simply a battle for your spirit. He wants to destroy your body, too, or at least pull you out of active duty for God. While many illnesses are not from Satan, others are. We must learn to be aware of his schemes and respond accordingly with prayer and faith.

Peace: "Shalom," a favorite Hebrew word of blessing, essentially means peace. When Psalm 128 concludes with "Peace be upon Israel," it means not just an absence of war, but a well-rounded life of joy, harmony, and prosperity. Satan opposes peace in the church; the family; and the individual, so he will use any ploy he can to upset a relationship. He'll aim a fiery dart with precision to inflame a petty difference. As long as the evil one can foment strife within a household, he has gained a foothold. He can then launch forays to prevent a husband and wife from showing their children and their acquaintances the love of Christ. Or he can handicap the parents so they move a child through his or her formative years without absorbing the Christian love, teaching, and example needed to be a healthy adult.

Faith: One of Satan's chief goals is persuading you to doubt his existence. If he succeeds there, why should you even believe in spiritual warfare? You have been rendered ineffective—of little consequence either to Satan or to God. If you know Satan is real, he'll work to convince you that God is vague, unresponsive to prayer, impotent, unconcerned with your trivial problems. If you believe that much, the father of lies will try to take you even further down the road of doubt, questioning God's very existence.

Reputation: If your reputation suffers because of sin or carelessness, you're probably getting what you deserve. However, even when you live a basically righteous life, Satan can always find others who will distort your most sincere motives and involvements. Satan especially wants to tarnish your reputation as a Christian, particularly if you have some degree of visibility. He knows that the world has an insatiable desire to gloat over hypocrisy, and the one duplicity that cannot be topped by politicians or financiers is the Christian who's preaching one thing and reaching for another.

Finances: So many people are prone to live beyond their means that you can't automatically attribute financial difficulty to satanic attack. Furthermore, we live in a fallen world where scarcity is a universal law. The earth simply does not hold enough of anything to begin to satisfy the needs and wants of humankind. We have all experienced that reality, no matter what tax bracket we fall in.

How can you discern if Satan is behind your financial difficulty? It's never easy, but through the practice of walking with God and resisting the devil, you gradually accumulate a sense of how and where Satan is resisting you. That's what happened with Mike and his wife. As they asked God to help them straighten out their priorities, one area that clearly stood out was finances. Mike was tempted to cut back on his tithing to apply more money toward their debts. His wife wisely cautioned against that strategy, and he heeded her advice. God's blessing came as promised in Scripture.

OFFSETTING THE RISKS

Indeed, our checkbooks speak loudly of our priorities. We see ourselves as masters of our households, being in complete control of our incomes, doling out dollars as we see fit. The Old Testament sheds a different light on tithing, referring to it as what "belongs to the Lord" (Leviticus 27:30), not something we bestow upon the Lord as a benefactor. Another passage says that we choose curse or blessing, depending on whether we choose to "rob" God of his tithe. It challenges us: "'Bring the whole tithe into the storehouse.... Test me in this,' says the Lord Almighty, 'and see if I will not throw open the floodgates of heaven and pour out so much blessing that you will not have room enough for it'" (Malachi 3:10).

The master deceiver will do everything in his power to blind men to the reality of tithing. Failing there, Satan will encourage the perspective that what you give to God and his work on the earth is not the first check you write, but the last. In that way, you will always feel pressure to compromise. You'll also forget that God's tenth was his to begin with, not yours.

Satan's strategy here is hardly limited to tithing. Whether he attacks our finances, health, inner peace, faith, or reputation, he always wants us to scramble around and draw upon our own strength, wisdom, and resources to shield our vulnerable areas. The devil wants us looking toward physicians and group insurance policies to solve our health problems, toward our good deeds and personal politicking to prop up our reputation.

Satan doesn't care if we offer a few superficial prayers, as long as we lack the long-term resolve not to wallow in worry and grasp for tangible solutions. God wants us to adopt a different perspective. Whether we're in the trenches, wounded and still ducking bullets, or temporarily resting in a bunker of strength, we can always benefit from this sound advice:

> Trust in the Lord with all your heart and lean not on your own understanding; in all your ways acknowledge him, and he will make your paths straight. Do not be wise in your own eyes; fear the Lord and shun evil. This will bring health to your body and nourishment to your bones. Honor the Lord with your wealth, with the firstfruits of all your crops; then your barns will be filled to overflowing, and your vats will brim over with new wine. My son, do not despise the Lord's discipline and do not resent his rebuke, because the Lord disciplines those he loves, as a father the son he delights in. **Proverbs 3:5-12**

Be humble and look to the Lord. Depend on his counsel and provision. Offer tithes to him. These steps become the starting point for physical health and financial prosperity. God isn't offering a short-cut to reaping spoils while dodging the draft for spiritual warfare. Rather, he describes the attitude required to qualify for active service.

As you consistently humble yourself and lean upon God, you will find it much easier to distinguish godly training and trials from demonic harassment. Unlike Satan's outright attacks, God's discipline has a noble purpose: to prepare you, his son, for the adult job of fighting for righteousness.

THE COSTS OF JOINING THE FRAY

A floor trader on the New York Stock Exchange understands the axiom that drives the market: buy low, sell high. The wise investor then takes his proceeds from selling high and buys low again.

Jesus advocated the same principle through some of his parables: Sell high (that is, what outwardly seems to be of great worth but really isn't) and use the proceeds to buy low (that is, what the world ignores but is really of supreme value). "The kingdom of heaven is like treasure hidden in a field. When a man found it, he hid it again, and then in his joy went and sold all he had and bought that field. Again, the kingdom of heaven is like a merchant looking for fine pearls. When he found one of great value, he went away and sold everything he had and bought it" (Matthew 13:44-46).

Jesus spoke to the issue of worldly wealth at other times as well. To the rich young ruler, he said, "Go, sell everything you have and give to the poor, and you will have treasure in heaven" (Mark 10:21). On another occasion, he taught, "What good will it be for a man if he gains the whole world, yet forfeits his soul? Or what can a man give in exchange for his soul?" (Matthew 16:26).

If the merchant sold *everything* in order to buy the fine pearls, is every Christian commanded to sell every last silver spoon and buy tickets for some mission field a dozen time zones away? No—though God has impressed that sort of message upon certain individuals. What, then, can we glean from these Scriptures? The Lord want us to have the right attitude about serving in his army: that we consider the cost to be *everything* we have. Every man must hold his possessions, his power and prestige, his hobbies, his private pleasures and rights, as if they were already sold and being loaned back to him by God, on a one-day renewal basis.

A war rages all around you, with or without your active involvement. You will do best to join the fray, but you can't be a good soldier encumbered by a five hundred-pound backpack. Having surrendered all that you own, you must be willing to travel light when necessary. It doesn't matter if you gain part of the world, or the whole ball of wax (and rock and water).

Whatever civilian loves you may have, lay them on the altar as a sacrifice. It's God's business whether he loans them back to you or consumes them with fire. Know what's worth giving up, and what's out there to be won.

THE SPOILS

So what exactly is there to be gained? Judging by the preceding Scriptures, you can expect:

The kingdom of heaven: a taste of God's harmonious order now and the fullness of heaven later.

Your soul: the reward of inner peace now, regardless of outward circumstances, and the promise of eternal life.

Treasure in heaven: the hope of good things awaiting you, a bounty proportional to the exercise of stewardship over what God has put under your authority on earth.

Satan will constantly blow smoke in your spiritual eyes. In your struggle between the things of this world and the things of the spirit, he wants you savoring only the glamorous baubles, the luxurious comforts, the soothing flattery—the very commodities that depreciate so fast they wouldn't buy a replacement string for your heavenly harp.

Instead, "Set your minds on things above, not on earthly things" (Colossians 3:2). God has given you the free will to direct your thoughts, your eyes, your desires. Wisely appraise what is of lasting value here and in heaven. Be willing to give up what has little value in the long run. Fight for what's worth gaining and forget the rest.

MASTER OR MARTYR?

Outside of the general promises listed in Scripture, no one can tell you exactly what you will get out of spiritual warfare.

Each battle is unique. Some battles you win; others you don't. Sometimes you're able to plunder the enemy and come away with your pockets stuffed with goodies. Other times you have to pay just to play or barely break even.

On the whole, you should eventually emerge victorious—*if* you're donning the armor of Ephesians 6 and wielding the sword of the spirit, the Word of God. You will likely have your eyes opened to increased hostility from Satan and his demons. Continually enter into deeper worship and prayer, and make the principles of normal Christian living part of your daily discipline. If you do, you should see the enemy increasingly retreat as God's power and integrity are manifest in whatever you touch.

You should also prosper on your job and be a more effective witness at work, as well as in all other social circles. You should begin to experience fellowship with God that is more like a friendship, with prayer more like a conversation with a very old and wise friend. If you're married, your relationship should begin to assume greater depth as you draw closer to each other and to God in resisting Satan's attacks. If you have children, you should see a godly order begin to form in their behavior, speech, and priorities.

I say "should" in all of these areas for good reason. God did not create a world governed by formulas. Suppose certain practices and beliefs were *guaranteed* to produce attraction between you and your wife, or repulsion between you and demons. Human beings would find it darn near impossible not to revere such principles—clearly a form of idolatry.

Instead, God created a world which is not so convenient and predictable, so neat and tidy. When you look at individual people, churches, political parties, situations, rarely do you find the black and white of pure good and pure evil. God's people are just as imperfect as anyone else. As they encounter spiritual struggles, they cannot bank on a particular outcome, no matter how righteous the cause. The guy on the white horse doesn't always ride off into the sunset after vanquishing the black villain. Even so, God desires to pour his light into that shadowy grayness. He waits for you to ask him to do so and is counting on you to be prepared when he acts.

THE JOY OF STANDING FIRM

Remember Shammah, the celebrated Hebrew warrior who stood his ground after his comrades has deserted him, who struck down the Philistines and achieved a great victory? Shammah embodies the admonition to don our spiritual armor: "Therefore put on the full armor of God, so that when the day of evil comes, you may be able to *stand* your ground, and after you have done everything, to *stand*. *Stand* firm then ..." (Ephesians 6:13-14).

The Greek words used here do not suggest a comprehensive assault against ruling principalities, as referred to in the verse just prior. Rather they speak more of individual soldiers simply holding their ground. What kind of soldier has Shammah-like staying power? He might not be particularly brave, but he's loyal. He might not be a fighter of superior skills, but he's prepared as best he can be. He might not remember the names of those who desert him, but he knows precisely who he is: a soldier with specific responsibilities and authority in the army of God.

That sure knowledge translates into identity—no small spoil to be gained from embracing the spiritual warfare that swirls around you. The difficulty of finding a valid identity plagues so many men, even if they prevail in work, sports, money, power, and sex. Yet God offers each man something more attainable, something profound in its simplicity: a field to defend, armor to wear, a sword for the attack, fellow soldiers with whom to share the battlefront, a kind and omniscient commander, and a remarkable book that serves as an exhaustive strategy manual, morale booster, history primer, and military forecaster (God's side wins, by the way).

You will find identity and inner peace in only one way: by standing firm in the field where God has placed you, and by engaging your individual battles, however small they may seem. And in that discovery, you will please the one who has called you to his service and perform no small part in advancing his kingdom.

Notes

ONE

Men of War

1. Geoffrey C. Ward, Ric Burns and Ken Burns, *The Civil War* (New York: Alfred A. Knopf, 1991), 70-72.
2. Ward, R. Burns, and K. Burns, 75-81.
3. Ward, R. Burns, and K. Burns, 67, 147, 138.
4. Ward, R. Burns, and K. Burns, 70.
5. Ward, R. Burns, and K. Burns, 138.
6. Ward, R. Burns, and K. Burns, 139-40.

TWO

Enemy Tactics

1. Larry Collins and Dominique Lapierre, *O Jerusalem!* (New York: Simon and Schuster, 1972), 210-12.
2. Jessie Penn-Lewis, *War on the Saints* (Fort Washington, Pennsylvania: The Christian Literature Crusade, 1977), 7.
3. Penn-Lewis, 8.

THREE

Portrait of the Male Warrior

1. Dr. James Dobson, "The Marriage Killers," *Focus on the Family* Magazine, February 1993, 6.
2. George Gilder, *Men and Marriage* (Gretna, Louisiana: Pelican Publishing Co., 1986), 5.

FOUR
Your Battle Gear

1. John R.W. Stott, *The Message of Ephesians* (Leicester, England: Inter-Varsity Press, 1979), 277.
2. John White, *The Fight* (Downers Grove, Illinois: InterVarsity Press, 1976), 69.
3. Stott, 282.

SEVEN
Sexual Sabotage

1. R. Kent Hughes, *Disciplines of a Godly Man* (Wheaton, Illinois: Crossway Books, 1991), 78-80.

ELEVEN
Exalt or Default?

1. Terry Law, *The Power of Praise and Worship* (Tulsa, Oklahoma: Victory House Publishers, 1985), 18-19.

TWELVE
Where Do You Fit in God's Battalion?

1. Charles H. Kraft, *Defeating Dark Angels* (Ann Arbor, Michigan: Servant Publications, 1992), 18.
2. Judith MacNutt, "Angels," *Charisma and Christian Life*, February 1993, 50.

THIRTEEN
Your Authority in Christ

1. R.C. Sproul, *Stronger than Steel* (San Francisco: Harper & Row, 1980), 57-73.

FIFTEEN
Hand-to-Hand Combat

1. Most of the material in these steps was compiled from Don Basham, "A New Look at Spiritual Warfare" (Mobile, Alabama: Compass Tapes, 1985).

Other Books of Interest
from Servant Publications

Life Passages for Men
Understanding the Stages of a Man's Life
E. James Wilder

Dr. E. James Wilder contends that many men never really grow up because they fail to successfully negotiate the difficult passage from boyhood to manhood. An almost equally tragic trend is the way many men in late middle age fail to make the transition to grandfathers and elders. The result is families and churches, and wider communities that are bereft of the leadership and stability older and wiser men can provide.

We must begin to understand the stages in a man's life, says Dr. Wilder, and teach our boys and men new and creative ways to negotiate the passage from one stage to the next. Then our boys will become men who can father and husband, and our older men wise and strong elders who will bless their families and the church.   *$8.99*

Father Hunger
Robert S. McGee

No matter what your father was like, chances are you long for a better relationship with him. The problem of father hunger affects not only our relationships with family and friends, it also deeply affects the way we think about God. With honesty and spiritual insight, McGee tackles this difficult issue in order to draw readers into a stronger and more confident relationship with their heavenly Father.   *$12.99*